Toronto Sketches 9

MIKE FILEY

Toronto Sketches

9

THE DUNDURN GROUP
TORONTO

Copy-Editor: Michael Carroll
Design: Andrew Roberts
Printer: Transcontinental

Library and Archives Canada Cataloguing in Publication

Filey, Mike, 1941–

   Toronto sketches 9 : "the way we were" / Mike Filey.

ISBN-10: 1-55002-613-5
ISBN-13: 978-1-55002-613-9

   1. Toronto (Ont.)--History. I. Title. II. Title: Toronto sketches nine.

FC3097.4.F5496 2006   971.3'541   C2006-900524-9

1 2 3 4 5   10   09   08   07   06

We acknowledge the support of the Canada Council for the Arts and the Ontario Arts Council for our publishing program. We also acknowledge the financial support of the Government of Canada through the Book Publishing Industry Development Program and The Association for the Export of Canadian Books, and the Government of Ontario through the Ontario Book Publishers Tax Credit program, and the Ontario Media Development Corporation.

Care has been taken to trace the ownership of copyright material used in this book. The author and the publisher welcome any information enabling them to rectify any references or credits in subsequent editions.

J. Kirk Howard, President

Printed and bound in Canada.
Printed on recycled paper.

www.dundurn.com

Dundurn Press	Gazelle Book Services Limited	Dundurn Press
3 Church Street, Suite 500	White Cross Mills	2250 Military Road
Toronto, Ontario, Canada	High Town, Lancaster, England	Tonawanda, NY
M5E 1M2	LA1 4XS	U.S.A. 14150

Table of Contents

Mike Filey's column "The Way We Were" has appeared in the *Toronto Sunday Sun* on a regular basis since 1975. Many of his earlier columns have been reproduced in volumes 1 through 8 of Dundurn Press's Toronto Sketches series. The columns in this book originally appeared in 2003 and 2004. Appended to each column is the date it first appeared as well as any relevant material that may have surfaced since that date (indicated by an asterisk).

The New Old Toronto Street

One of the most historic streets in Toronto is little Toronto Street. It's only one block long, if you don't count the intersection it makes on the east side with Court Street, another small thoroughfare that also has some interesting history. To further define the limits of the present-day Toronto Street, it connects King Street to the south with Adelaide to the north. Notice that I used the expression "the present-day Toronto Street," since what we have today is not the Toronto Street originally laid out by a few pioneer surveyors back in the late 1700s.

Historically, today's Toronto Street is, in relative terms, a rather recent addition that came into being sometime after 1830. Dr. Scadding in his book *Toronto of Old* identifies the original Toronto Street as today's Victoria Street, and a very busy street it was. That's because in the early days of York (Toronto's original name), Yonge Street did not extend south of Lot Street (now Queen) due to the presence of a marshy swamp. Back then the small community's "downtown" was along King Street east and west of Church Street. To get there pedestrians as well as animal-drawn wagons and carts from the north and northwest would have to detour around the marsh and continue the trip via a thoroughfare called Toronto Street that connected Lot with King.

When it was decided to fill in the marsh and extend Yonge Street south of Queen, the original Toronto Street was closed and that land

Looking north on Toronto Street from the same vantage point on King Street in 1914 and in 2002.

given to those who owned property through which the newly length-ened Yonge Street now ran. By the way, it should be noted that back then opening and closing roads was no big deal since in most cases these so-called "roads" were usually no more that dirt paths.

Some years later a new street was opened east of Victoria that con-nected King with Adelaide. To identify it an old street name was res-urrected. It became today's Toronto Street. Several grand buildings were erected on the new street only a couple of which still exist. They can be seen in the accompanying photos taken from the same vantage point and separated in time by more than 90 years.

To the extreme left is the Seventh Toronto Post Office (1851–53), a Greek temple-like structure now occupied by the Argus Corporation. Still on the left and at the top of the street is the Excelsior Life Building erected in 1914–15 and designed by "Old" City Hall architect E.J. Lennox. Opposite it, and barely visible in the modern photo, is the Consumers' Gas Building (erected 1876, with an 1899 addition).

At the top of the street in the old photo is the Eighth Toronto Post Office of 1876. It was sacrificed in 1960 for the modern office building that looms in the background of the 2002 view. For transportation buffs, the old view features a horse and wagon, a couple of bicycles, and a half-dozen or so of the new-fangled gas buggies.

January 5, 2003

Bridging the Western Gap

So there I was reading one of Toronto's newspapers when I came across another of those articles concerning the building of a bridge from the foot of Bathurst Street over the Western Gap to Toronto Island. This one had some interesting comments that I thought the reader would find of interest.

> While on a recent tour around the harbour, the chairman of the Toronto Harbour Commission stated that the work of constructing a bridge connecting the city and the Island at the foot of Bathurst Street should be started at once.
>
> "How would you finance it?" he was asked.
>
> "I believe that the Dominion and Provincial governments, the city and the Harbour Commission should contribute to its construction," he replied.
>
> "And what about the objections raised by the Island residents that it would mean cars over there?"
>
> "I have only this to say, that the Island is for all the citizens, and not for a few."

With the Island bridge very much in the news these days, one might conclude that this article appeared in a recent edition of the newspaper. However, eagle-eyed readers will no doubt have noticed references to the "Toronto Harbour Commission" and the use of the expression "Dominion government" in the article. The former vanished in 1999 with the creation of the new Toronto Port Authority, and the infrequent use of the word *Dominion* these days provides clues that the news item as quoted is an old one. But how old you may ask?

It actually appeared in the *Telegram* on April 1, 1924! And mercy me, they're still haggling over the project.

Actually the idea of connecting the Island to the mainland is much older than that. In fact, we find that building such a bridge was one of the conditions attached to allowing streetcars to operate on Sundays in Toronto.

In this day of wide-open Sundays it's difficult to believe that at one time in Toronto's past the operation of public transit vehicles of any kind on Sunday was illegal, and those who tried to do so could and would be fined and/or put in jail. And with the adoption of the Lord's Day Act in the early 1900s other things that we now take for granted (buying bread, participating in sports, going to the movies) were also defined as being against the law.

This streetcar is typical of the kind that would have been used on the proposed Toronto Island route over the Western Gap. The sides were removed during the warmer months, resulting in these vehicles being known as "convertible cars." This particular vehicle, seen here at the Dovercourt and Van Horne (now Dupont) intersection in 1904, was built 10 years earlier and scrapped in 1925.

In the case of Sunday streetcars, arguments were made both pro and con for their operation with a series of referendum votes being called to settle the question. The votes in 1892 and again in 1893 saw the use of the cars on the Sabbath defeated, while that of 1897 resulted in the operation of Sunday streetcars approved by a margin of slightly more than 200 out of a total of 32,324 cast. It was close, but Torontonians were now able to go to church on a streetcar.

Part of the scheme put forward by the privately owned streetcar company to influence the approval of the lucrative Sunday streetcar operations was its agreement to establish a new streetcar route to the Island. This line, which would be part of the city system accessible from any other city route using a transfer, would permit the less-affluent Toronto population a day on the Island without the necessity of paying the extra 10-cent fare to cross the bay on a privately owned ferry boat.

The street railway company, while appearing to be on the side of the general public, knew that there was little likelihood of ever having to build this line since the cost of erecting a bridge over the Western Gap on which the tracks would be laid as well as the access road from Bathurst and King streets were the sole responsibilities of the city. It was a well-known fact that the cash-strapped young city didn't have an extra $104,720 lying around for something as frivolous as a bridge to the Island.

By the way, today's estimated cost of building an Island bridge, now referred to as a "fixed link," has increased somewhat and is now estimated at many millions of dollars.

January 12, 2003

Transporting Toronto

L ocated just north of the city's busy waterfront and steps from the CN Tower and SkyDome is the ancient CP Roundhouse. Where Canadian Pacific Railway's mighty steam engines were once serviced, the folks at Steam Whistle Brewery now turn out a tasty Pilsner.

While it's good to see somebody occupying what was just another abandoned historic building, a brewery certainly wasn't what many of us hoped would be the fate of the old structure that was constructed in 1929 on the site of Canadian Pacific's first Toronto roundhouse.

Steam engines continued to be serviced in this unique building for more than half a century with the huge doors closing for good in 1986. After the building's closure, I remember attending meeting after meeting during which a multitude of interested and well-meaning people discussed a whole bunch of ideas that might bring the old building back to life. Some believed that an operating steam railway museum would be the perfect re-use while others, myself included, thought that it would be a great place to tell the much broader story of Canada's fascinating transportation history.

Our plan would include, but not be limited to, just the era of steam. Showing the world what Canadians have done on land and sea and in the air would, we believed, do more to maximize visitations and increase income.

Souvenir postcard of the Toronto-built passenger steamer SS *Kingston*. Note the biplane overhead.

But those discussions ultimately went for naught when in the late spring of 2000 Steam Whistle began brewing operations in the roundhouse. Since that time any ideas to use the rest of the building for museum purposes seem to have been deleted from the old building's future role in Toronto.

That's unfortunate because there's quite a story to tell. Any plan to tell the country's transportation story in a roundhouse setting certainly wouldn't lack for content. In fact, you could use all of the building's massive interior space just to tell the story of Toronto's contributions to that fabulous story.

For instance, here are just two events that took place in Toronto on January 19, the day I originally wrote this column, that prove my point.

It was on a cold January 19, 1901, that one of the finest passenger lake boats ever seen on the Great Lakes was launched in Toronto. And on that same date, a mere 49 years later, the first all-Canadian fighter jet designed and built in this country took to the skies out at the Avro Canada plant northwest of Toronto.

There is no question that January 19 was, and remains, a special day in the history of transportation in Ontario's capital.

The steamer *Kingston* was built for the Richelieu and Ontario Navigation Company (R&O) by the Bertram Engineering Works whose shipyard was located at the foot of Bathurst Street. The factory where parts of the great ship were fabricated is now occupied, in part, by the exotic car dealership at the northeast corner of Front and Bathurst. The finished components were transported across the railway tracks, down to the waterfront where they would be fitted together in time to create a fine new passenger ship, the 290-foot-long SS *Kingston*, which was powered by an inclined, three-crank, triple-expansion steam engine that ran a pair of 23-foot-diameter side paddlewheels. *Kingston* operated on the Toronto–Thousand Islands–Prescott run. At that last port most passengers would transfer to other ships for the thrilling ride through the Lachine Rapids and onwards to Montreal.

However, following the tragic and deadly fire of September 17, 1949, that destroyed SS *Noronic* while at its berth in Toronto, Canada Steamship Lines (the successor to the R&O) decided to end all passenger ship service. The once-proud *Kingston* was retired from service and eventually scrapped.

Interestingly, even while this Toronto-built vessel awaited its fate, another creation from the hands of a new generation of local craftsman was about to make Canadian aviation history. With the world immersed in the uncertainties of the Cold War, the Royal Canadian Air Force was searching for a new aircraft to replace its outdated collection of piston-engine Mustangs and Sea Furies and

Avro Canada's second CF-100, FB-K, designed and built at the company's suburban Toronto factory.

pioneer Vampire jets. What was needed was an all-purpose, all-weather, twin-engine jet fighter.

Officials looked at a number of jets designed and built by Americans, but decided our people could do as well or even better. This decision, one that was derided at the time by several so-called experts, would result in Avro Canada's remarkable CF-100, the first of which flew January 19, 1950.

In total, 692 CF-100s were built at the Malton, Ontario, factory. Interestingly, even after 30 years had passed since that first flight, several of the aircraft were still active as electronic warfare trainers. One CF-100 has even been honoured in the form of a permanent monument in a park-like setting on Derry Road East (near Goreway Drive), just a short distance from its birthplace.

To learn more about this Canadian aviation success story (and one that could have been a feature attraction in Canada's transportation story in the CP Roundhouse) read The *Avro CF-100* by Larry Milberry from CANAV Books.

January 19, 2003

---

* After the sale of SkyDome to Rogers Communications in early 2005, the name of the stadium was quickly changed to Rogers Centre.

Bright, Shiny, and New

Almost without exception this column features an "ancient" photograph more often than not taken by some anonymous photographer. To be sure, where the identity of the person who took the picture is known the work is credited. Unfortunately, the passage of time since the photo was snapped usually precludes that possibility.

The matter of photo credits aside, in almost every instance where there are buildings in the old photograph, the vast majority of those structures has been demolished as a result of Toronto's rush to replace what many regarded as passé, with things bright, shiny, and new.

One conclusion that might be drawn from all of this is that any photo containing an image of a building that no longer stands must have been taken by an old (or deceased) photographer. With this in mind you can imagine my consternation as I went through a bunch of photographs that I personally took since acquiring my interest in old Toronto some years ago. Many of those views showed buildings that are no more. Can it be that my stuff is also "ancient"? Is it possible that I am getting old? Or am I just older?

While I sit back and ponder my future I offer for your perusal a quartet of my "ancient" photos.

January 26, 2003

The University Theatre stood on the north side of Bloor Street between Bellair Street and Avenue Road. This was one of the first major motion picture palaces to be erected following the end of the Second World War in 1945. The 1,556-seat theatre's official opening was postponed several times owing to the shortage of structural steel that had been diverted for use in the construction of electrical generating stations around the province. This same shortage resulted in the delayed opening of the Toronto-Barrie highway (now 400) and the Toronto Bypass Highway (now 401). The University finally opened in 1949 and was one of the city's most popular movie houses until its closure in 1986. At that time there were plans to incorporate a portion of the theatre as well as the theatre facade in the new development planned for the site. Unfortunately, the curtain never went up on this interesting proposal. The marquee reveals that the feature presentation at the theatre when I took this picture in 1979 was *Apocalypse Now*.

When I was a kid, this imposing structure was usually referred to rather disparagingly as "999 Queen Street." Built between 1846 and 1858, the Provincial Lunatic Asylum was regarded as one of the most modern treatment facilities for the mentally ill anywhere in the world. Unfortunately, the stigma of what went on inside the asylum precluded the building having any future. And while pleas were made to at least save certain architecturally significant portions of the complex (the massive dome, for instance), the whole thing came crashing down in 1975. The Queen Street Mental Health Centre now occupies the site.

While on the subject of unimposing buildings (actually this structure still stands or was standing when I wrote this article), this building at the southeast corner of Dupont Street and Westmoreland Avenue is where Torontonian Norman Breakey perfected his Koton Koter in the early 1940s. Where who perfected his what? Norman Breakey was the inventor of the paint roller that Eaton's and Simpson's sold under the name Koton Koter for $1.98. Following a typically Canadian scenario, Norman wasn't able to raise sufficient funds to protect his invention and soon variations of his creation had flooded the market, leaving poor Mr. Breakey as a might-have-been millionaire.

Constructed in the early 1900s to house the "Northern" branch of the Traders' Bank of Canada, this imposing building on the north-east corner of Yonge and Bloor became a branch of the Royal Bank when the latter took over the former in 1912. It was demolished to clear the way for the unimposing Hudson's Bay Centre that opened in 1974.

An Elegant Liquor Store

Located on the east side of Yonge Street, halfway between Davenport Road and St. Clair Avenue, is the former CPR North Toronto Station. Once regarded as a component of the city's fast-growing passenger steam railroad network, the building saw its importance as a transportation hub vanish soon after the opening of Toronto's new Union Station downtown on Front Street West.

Deprived of its passengers, the once-proud structure with its landmark clock tower was eventually converted to other uses. Perhaps it was its newfound popularity as a combination beer and liquor store that precluded any chance of its demolition, an irreversible fate that many of the building's contemporaries had met. Whatever the reason, the station survived and re-opened in February 2003 as the site of Canada's largest (and might I add most elegant) liquor store.

Interestingly, the reason that the CPR opened the new North Toronto Station in 1916 was actually nothing more than an act of defiance. The company, as well as the nation's other two transcontinental railways, the Canadian Northern and Grand Trunk, had been ordered by the federal government to construct and help pay for a modern new railway station to replace the city's outdated 1872 Union Station that was located on the south side of Front opposite today's University Avenue. In addition to the cost of the new station the railways were also expected to help pay for a new viaduct and the associated bridges and underpasses that would be required to allow the trains unobstructed access to and from the station.

The estimated cost of the project was $28.5 million, and officials of the CPR eventually decided they wanted no part of it. They would build their own station instead. And it would be far uptown, adjacent to the company's cross-town main line.

It's summer 1916, and the CPR's new North Toronto Station awaits its first visitors. The tower clock tells us it's 10:00 a.m.

This decision having been made the company then hired the prestigious Toronto architectural firm of Darling and Pearson to design the new station. The first set of drawings was altered when it was decided that the Canadian Northern would use the same facility. Finally, on September 9, 1915, Toronto's popular mayor Tommy Church tapped the station's cornerstone into place.

The mayor was back a little more than nine months later to officially open the new $250,000 station. Within weeks of the opening approximately 10 trains a day were calling at the new CP North Toronto Station.

Still a stately building, even though the clock has long since vanished, the station awaits its future in this photo I took more than a decade ago.

The Canadian Northern wouldn't use the station very long, though. It, along with several other financially embarrassed railways including the Grand Trunk, were taken over by the federal government and combined into the new Canadian National Railways.

Before long the new North Toronto Station was overcrowded, but the company still refused to get involved in the new waterfront station. Rumours started to circulate that the CPR had acquired a large parcel of land close to where Maple Leaf Gardens now stands on Carlton Street, just east of Yonge. The rumours suggested that it would be here that CPR would build a mammoth new underground railway terminal of its own complete with a huge hotel soaring high above the proposed station. A 100-foot-wide tunnel would be built through the terminal, and trains would be brought to the proposed new downtown terminal from the main line at the existing North Toronto Station. Of course, it was all rumours.

Eventually, CPR officials thought better of their decision not to be part of the majestic new Union Station on Front Street, and by late 1929 CPR trains were operating out of the new facility. Meanwhile, the North Toronto Station, now devoid of any railway traffic, soon took on a new role as the site of beer and liquor outlets.

The building has suffered over the past few decades, but now with its facade and interior all nicely cleaned up and its 140-foot-high tower featuring a clock once more, the CPR North Toronto Station is a shining example of what can be done with our city landmarks if someone cares.

February 2, 2003

Car Show on the Road Again

The Canadian International Car Show is one of Canada's most popular consumer exhibitions. It usually takes place at the Toronto Convention Centre on Front Street West, where at least 300,000 visitors are wowed, dazzled, and amazed by the hundreds of cars, trucks, and specialty vehicles on display.

Newspaper records seem to be unanimous in the conclusion that the first gasoline-powered "horseless carriages" seen on Toronto's frequently dusty, often muddy streets were those driven by anonymous American visitors who crossed the rather porous border on exploration trips into what many of them still referred to simply as British North America.

Incidentally, the term *gasoline-powered* is important in this story since once the visitors got here they would probably have seen a local patent attorney, one Frederick Fetherstonhaugh, roaming the city streets in a "battery-powered" machine built for him in the small Yonge Street factory of inventor William Still. By the way, that vehicle, the battery of which was recharged using power from the overhead of the Toronto and York Radial Railway that ran in front of Mr. Fetherstonhaugh's place on Lake Shore Road near today's Royal York Road, was still in service more than a decade later.

As for the first Canadian to own a gas-powered auto, there's little doubt that the honour belongs to Hamilton, Ontario's John Moodie.

He purchased an American-built one-cylinder Winton on April 2, 1898, from none other than Alexander Winton, the company president who travelled to the Steel City from his Cleveland plant to conclude the deal in person. It's been suggested that had Moodie made his acquisition one day sooner he would have been the purchaser of the first gas-powered car on the continent.

An awesome array of new vehicles awaits the crowds that will visit the 1929 edition of the National Motor Show of Canada held on the two floors of Simpson's Arcadian Court in downtown Toronto.

Nevertheless, Moodie's new car had cost him $1,000, but as usual there was still the duty to be paid. The customs people classified the strange vehicle as a "carriage" on which the duty was 35 percent. Moodie insisted that the car should be regarded as a "locomotive." Moodie eventually won his case (the last in history to do so) thereby saving himself 100 bucks. Moodie didn't keep the car very long, selling it to Torontonian Dr. Perry Doolittle, who then claimed the distinction of being the purchaser of Canada's first used car.

Doolittle, who is buried in Toronto's Mount Pleasant Cemetery, is an interesting person in his own right. He became a major player in the development of both cars and highways throughout the Dominion and was one of the founders of what we know today as the Canadian Automobile Association. He was also the first person (with friend Edward Flickenger) to drive a vehicle (a 1926 Model T Ford) from coast to coast under its own power, although for part of the trip flanged steel wheels replaced the car's rubber tires to allow the vehicle to travel over railway tracks through otherwise inaccessible areas.

As the years went by, an ever-increasing number of vehicles from a wide variety of manufacturers began to appear on city streets, and it wasn't long before impromptu "car shows" erupted on the side of the road as curious crowds gathered around the latest models. Every so often, local automobile dealers filled their showrooms with different models they had the rights to sell and then advertised the event as a "car show." However, the first time that an "all-models" event was held, not just in Toronto but anywhere in the entire country, occurred on March 31, 1906, when the Canadian Automobile and Boat Show opened in the covered rink in the rear of the old Granite Club on Church Street (a portion of which still stands as 519 Church Street).

Other Toronto venues for automobile shows over the ensuing years were the Armouries on University Avenue (now the site of the Court House) and the Transportation (destroyed by fire in 1974) and Horticultural (still standing) buildings at the Canadian National Exhibition. So important were these shows that in 1929 a building dedicated specifically to cars and trucks was built at the east end of the CNE grounds. It was here that the newest models were first seen by the Canadian public attending the fall fair. Unfortunately, when the CNE decided to move its show dates from early September to late August, the only vehicles available for display were the previous year's models. As this was of little use to the dealers or of interest to the public, the last of the once extremely popular CNE car shows was held in 1967.

One of the most unusual venues ever selected for a car show in Toronto was the one chosen for the February 1929 edition of the National Motor Show of Canada. Its exhibition hall was none other than Simpson's magnificent two-storey Arcadian Court on the eighth and ninth floors of the store's recently completed Bay Street addition. To get the cars into place, they had to be hoisted up the Richmond Street side of the building and hauled in through the windows. No doubt quite a sight. After the car show, the Arcadian Court would be advertised as the largest restaurant in a department store anywhere in the world.

February 9, 2003

Attitude Adjustment

It's funny how our values change with the passage of time. Attitudes towards the preservation of historic structures are a case in point. I can recall that during the initial discussions back in 1965 about something called the Eaton Centre many people believed that this futuristic $260-million project was just too important to Toronto, and to the future of its downtown, to allow anything, anything, to jeopardize its completion. And since the original version of the Centre was to occupy the entire Queen, Bay, Dundas, Yonge parcel of land, the demolition of virtually every building standing on that property was pretty much a foregone conclusion regardless of any historic significance any of those structures might have had.

For sure, all the shops on the west side of Yonge from Dundas to Queen would go except for the old Woolworth store at the Yonge and Queen corner. That wasn't because of any specific historical significance. No, it was because the site was owned by McMaster University as a result of an ancient will drawn up by a member of the Bilton family who didn't like Timothy Eaton very much. As a result, the site was off-limits to anyone connected with the Eatons. I wonder if that will is still in force.

The future of several other buildings in what was being referred to as the "superblock," including the Salvation Army headquarters, the historic 1847 Holy Trinity Anglican Church, and a couple of the church's neighbouring buildings, also appeared to be in jeopardy. But there was one structure on the site that many Torontonians regarded as untouchable. That was Toronto's "Old" City Hall, a building that had stood at the northeast corner of Queen and Bay since 1899 (although back then the stretch of Bay north of Queen was still called Terauley).

"Old" City Hall was once regarded as one of the finest municipal buildings on the continent, and the decision by City Council not to turn it over to the developers was one of the main reasons for the failure of that first Eaton Centre proposal. In fact, recog-nizing how important the old building was to the outcome of the discussions, the developers even went as far as to suggest they would keep the 300-foot-high clock tower and the Cenotaph as gestures of goodwill. But, nope, it was the preservation of the entire building or the deal was off. Sentiment and fiscal conflicts won the day, and on May 18, 1967, Eaton Centre Number 1 was officially declared dead.

Some of the original carved sandstone gargoyles near the top of the tower are visible in this circa 1910 photo of today's "Old" City Hall.

In early 1971, plans for a revised version of the Eaton Centre were presented to city officials. With the old expression "once bitten, twice shy" in mind, this time the modified design didn't come anywhere near "Old" City Hall. But this proposal was also to face intensive scrutiny before the first building permits were issued. Finally, after more than 12 years of discussions, Phase 1A, consisting of 150 shops and a new main store for Eaton's, Toronto's new (and revised) Eaton Centre opened on February 10, 1977. The rest of the project, referred to as Phase 1B, opened on August 8, 1979. Since then the Centre has had several "facelifts" as it continues to be one of Toronto's top attractions.

Now, here's the most interesting part of the long, long Eaton Centre saga. When the original scheme for the Centre was proposed in 1965, it looked as if "Old" City Hall was doomed. But the rally cry went out, and for a variety of reasons, including those of financial and sentimental merit, the ancient landmark was spared. Not only spared, but the city's change in attitude towards its few remaining historic treasures has resulted in a long-term, multimillion-dollar plan being initiated to ensure that "Old" City Hall remains a part of the city landscape well into the future.

By the time this postcard view was published, the gargoyles had been removed.

Under the direction of City of Toronto officials, Ventin Group (Toronto), Inc., is in the process of supervising the restoration of much of the badly weathered brick and stones (and related masonry work). Included in the project is the installation of new copper roofing and something that most people had forgotten about — the re-appearance of the four gargoyles near the top of the clock tower. These unusual features, which were originally carved out of sandstone, had been removed years ago as a safety measure. However, the present restoration program is so meticulous that the scary foursome are back in place though now cast in bronze.

February 16, 2003

Wind in Their Sails

There's a myriad of attractions to be seen at the century-plus-old Canadian National Exhibition, but one exhibit has year-round appeal combining, as it does, the age-old concept of using wind to do work and the more recent theory of having that same wind generate electricity.

And that's exactly what the 308-foot-high windmill (technically, its called a wind turbine) at the west end of Exhibition Grounds is doing as its trio of 95-foot-long blades spin at a maximum 21 revolutions per minute. In fact, the electrical output of this one turbine is sufficient to supply the needs of approximately 250 households. Actually, that statement is rather simplistic. What really happens is that the power generated by the Windshare wind turbine is fed into the city's electrical grid where it helps decrease the total amount of power needed to serve the community. As a result, the more turbines, the fewer kilowatts of power required from other sources. For more details about this interesting project, see the *www.trec.on.ca/windshare* website.

While the windmill (aka, wind turbine) down at Exhibition Grounds is certainly a newer feature on Toronto's skyline, it isn't the city's first such structure. The honour for that goes to the windmill erected in the fall of 1832 at the edge of Toronto Bay just east of the foot of Parliament Street. That one was made of brick (105,000 of them to be exact), was 70 feet high, and was an important component of new arrival James Worts's new business enterprise.

Worts had immigrated to York (Toronto) in 1831 from Suffolk, England, in search of a new home for his family as well as for his brother-in-law William Gooderham and offspring. James selected the tiny town of little more than 3,000 souls nestled on the shore of a small bay protected from the often raging waters of Lake Ontario by the curving arm of a peninsula (that, following a fierce storm on April 13, 1858, was transformed into what we now refer to as Toronto Island).

James was familiar with wind-powered gristmills, having operated one back in Suffolk where winds off the North Sea provided the power to turn the sails to grind the grain. Worts was sure that winds off Lake Ontario, caught by fabric sails, would provide the power to turn grinding stones. So he went ahead and built his new wind-powered gristmill on the shoreline at the southeast corner of the town site.

The Windshare wind turbine at Exhibition Place. The 1930 Shriners' Peace Monument is in the foreground.

With a successful wheat-grinding business now virtually assured, James contacted William back in England and suggested that he and the rest of the Wortses and Gooderhams come to live in York. William agreed, and when the brood arrived in the summer of 1832, the contingent that consisted of family members, servants, and 11 orphans increased the population of little York by a total of 54.

Tragically, just two years after the families had nicely settled in York, James Worts, despondent over his wife's death during childbirth, ended it all by throwing himself down the company's well. It was then that William Gooderham brought a nephew into the business, and from then on what had been Worts and Gooderham became Gooderham and Worts.

While the milling business always made money for the young

enterprise, by 1837 a better income was being realized from the distilling of surplus and second-grade grain into whiskey. With the sources of most drinking water suspect, whiskey (and beer) were the beverages of choice, both having received some form of sterilization in their manufacture. In short order Gooderham and Worts became the largest distilling operation (and the largest taxpayer) in the entire country.

The Worts and Gooderham windmill on the York (Toronto) shoreline, circa 1832.

Oh, that pioneer windmill — its use was abandoned when the company turned to steam power, and the windmill was demolished in 1858. In 1954 a scaled-down version of the old windmill was erected near the corner of Front and Parliament streets using bricks from a razed structure of the same period. This windmill, too, was destroyed, having been built where a support for the new elevated Gardiner Expressway was planned.

March 2, 2003

On the Toronto Waterfront

Over time what had started out as a rather simple flour mill and windmill operated by William Gooderham and his son, James, evolved into one of the largest distilleries in North America. Many of the firm's original buildings are now undergoing restoration for a number of new uses.

Interestingly, the original Worts and Gooderham windmill served another purpose, one that bore no relation to either milling or distilling. It formed the eastern end of an imaginary line drawn on an 1832 map of the harbour by city officials connecting the site of the old distillery windmill with the ruins of the French fort (Fort Rouillé) that stood for less than a decade steps west of the present-day Bandshell in Exhibition Place (and coincidentally steps east of the new wind turbine).

The boundary resulted from concerns that wharves would be extended farther and farther into the bay to take advantage of additional loading and off-loading space. This extra space would translate into additional income for the wharf owner while severely inconveniencing the hundreds of ships arriving and departing the busy Port of Toronto each sailing season. To offset this possibility the Windmill Line would delineate the maximum southerly limit of any wharf constructed from the mainland out into Toronto Bay.

The original 1832 Windmill Line was extended farther south into the bay on several occasions with the final adjustment made in 1893.

As the rules on how far south into the bay Toronto's waterfront could be extended changed, so, too, did the look of the central waterfront. In the foreground is an area of newly reclaimed land created by dumping hundreds of tons of fill at the foot of Yonge Street.

The same view a decade later. Large portions of the newly reclaimed land have been paved over and new streets such as Fleet and Harbour (each now part of Lake Shore Boulevard), lower Yonge Street, and Queen's Quay opened. The new skyscraper in town is the recently completed Bank of Commerce Building on the south side of King Street, a block west of Yonge.

Looking north on Yonge Street from Toronto Bay in 2002.

Each change resulted in the filling in of the water lots between wharves and the creation of acres of new land along the water's edge. In 1925 the historic Windmill Line was superseded by the Toronto Harbour Commission's new Harbourhead Line, which defines the waterfront configuration of today.

March 9, 2003

Send in the Cavalry

John Marteison's *Second to None* is a wonderful book published by Robin Brass Studios. In an easy-to-read text accompanied by dozens of rare and contemporary photographs, it details the fascinating history of the Governor General's Horse Guards, one of Canada's proudest military regiments. The regiment traces its lineage back to the earliest days of Ontario when in 1798 John Button, an American-born Loyalist, arrived in the Province of Upper Canada (Ontario). He settled in what is now the Town of Markham, where the name of the pretty little community of Buttonville continues to honour his memory.

Button established the province's first cavalry unit, which served with distinction along the Niagara frontier during the War of 1812 as well as in the defence of Toronto (then called York) during the American invasion in the spring of 1813. It was during the Rebellion of 1837 that Button's Troop joined forces with another local militia group under the command of George Taylor Denison, the progenitor of one of Toronto's most influential families. A host of Denison names, birthplaces, and local homesteads is recorded in the titles of many city streets: Bellevue, Ossington, Dovercourt (correctly spelled Dover Court), Rusholme, Major, Robert, Lippincott, and little Rolyat (Taylor spelled backwards).

In 1853 these two cavalry units were combined to form the First Regiment York Light Dragoons. In 1866 royal assent was given to another change resulting in the name Governor General's Bodyguard.

Seventy years later this regiment amalgamated with the Mississauga Horse (another proud city regiment that had been gazetted in 1904) to become the Governor General's Horse Guards. During its existence, in addition to service in the War of 1812 and the rebellious times of 1837, the regiment was active in the Fenian Raids of 1866, the 1885 North-West Rebellion, the South African War, two world wars, and the Korean conflict for which the Horse Guards recruited 223 men, the most of any Canadian militia unit.

Members of the Governor General's Bodyguard parade at the Armouries on the east side of University Avenue, circa 1912. The name Armoury Street reminds us of this once-proud building through which thousands marched on their way overseas to defend freedom. Regrettably, the historic old structure was demolished in 1963.

* * *

That shuffling noise you're hearing is the sound of thousands of Toronto Maple Leafs fans either getting on or getting off the band-wagon. One day the team's a winner, going all the way. The next day, they're a bunch of bums. But love 'em or hate 'em, they're ours.

For me, a Leafs fan since that first game in 1941 played just days after I was born at old Grace Hospital on Bloor Street, it's hard to believe that in such a hockey-mad community as Toronto one would have to be pushing 40 to have even been around when the city last won the coveted Stanley Cup. Nevertheless, hope springs eternal, and yes, I'll say it, this is our year. Or maybe it will be next year, or the next ...

Actually, March 16, the day this column first appeared, is an important date in the long and illustrious history of the Toronto Maple Leafs. On that date the team under coach Howie Meeker set a record that still stands. It was during one of those good old-fashioned Saturday night games when the National Hockey League was still made up of a mere half-dozen teams (and you could actually see the players' faces) that our guys plastered the Rangers from New York 14–1. That was (and still is) the most goals scored by a Leafs team in one game. As great a feat as that was, it didn't help. The team finished fifth that year and out of the playoffs.

Nevertheless, here are some names from that March 16, 1957, game that will bring back happy hockey memories for many. Hat tricks against the Rangers' goalie "Gump" Worsley were scored by Brian Cullen and Sid Smith, with Tod Sloan and Ron Stewart scoring a pair each. Singles went to Al MacNeil, George Armstrong, Dick Duff, and Rudy Migay. The only Leafs who didn't score at least one point in that memorable game were Jim Thompson and goalie Ed Chadwick.

Here's another interesting fact about that particular match. Its outcome was reported in one city newspaper a full day before any of the other papers told the story. Why? Because the Sunday following the game, March 17, 1957, was the day Toronto finally got a Sunday newspaper, in this case the *Sunday Telegram*. Well ahead of its time (the first *Sunday Sun* didn't appear for another 16 years), the idea of a Sunday newspaper was too "radical" for the times and the *Sunday Telegram* lasted less than a year.

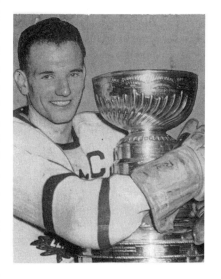

Ted "Teeder" Kennedy was the captain of the Toronto Maple Leafs team that scored 14 goals on March 16, 1957, the most scored by a Leafs squad in one game. Here he is hugging the Stanley Cup when the Leafs were 1950–51 champions. By the way, when was the last time you saw a Leaf hug the Stanley Cup? Or are you still waiting?

March 16, 2003

Sightseeing Chariots

I n this modern day and age, and in the hustle and bustle of everyday activities, most Torontonians haven't the time to consider their morning or evening streetcar as a sightseeing chariot from which to gaze upon "the wonders that are Toronto."

Well, that may be exaggerating things a bit, but that's how the tourist brochures were describing the new-fangled electric vehicles in the 1890s. And there was no more popular route than the one known as the Belt Line. It encircled the downtown part of the city, in both directions, using track on King, Sherbourne, Bloor, and Spadina. What follows is a verbatim description of a spring excursion along the Belt Line in May 1897. Where appropriate I have added, in square brackets, a few of my own comments.

> The mildest form of excursion in which the citizens of Toronto indulge is a "ride on the Belt Line." After the hour of the evening meal on these warm nights by what seems common impulse they sally forth and intercept at some point of its wide circuit this most popular of street railway routes. The keenest competition exists for front place upon the open cars, out of the glare of the electric light and in full current of the breeze, in the sultriest weather created by the rapid movement. All sorts of conditions of humanity are patrons: nor does the rich man disdain to spend and repent

the humble fare [adults five cents, children three cents] for the sake of the interest, amusement, variety of scene and refreshment the trip affords. The stranger within our gates, of whom we shall have many this season, can use no better and no cheaper means of viewing the city, and within an hour seeing, catching sight alone, perchance, of our chief public buildings, our churches and finest residential and business streets.

The Belt Line covers a distance of seven miles. Boarding a car at the corner of King and Yonge streets and proceeding eastwards, the passenger may first glance up Toronto street, at the head of which the post office [demolished] stands flanked by buildings devoted to the legal brotherhood. At Church street St. James's Cathedral looks from its lofty, grey, serene old height upon the small traffic of men. At its feet are cool gardens and the wayfarer may stray within. North of it is the unadorned facade of the Public Library [northeast corner Adelaide, demolished] where wisdom is more esteemed than a brown stone front. At Jarvis street an old landmark is passed in St. Lawrence [Hall and] Market, and south of it may be seen the small dome of the City Hall [1844–1899] soon to be superseded by the magnificent buildings on Queen street, not in vision from the route.

The "run" north on Sherbourne street is accounted the prettiest portion of the Belt Line. All Saints Church [southeast corner] is passed and at Gerrard street the spacious well-kept Horticultural [Allen] Gardens cover one block. At the [southeast] corner of Carlton street the Sherbourne Street Methodist Church is situated and higher up on the west side is [the Roman Catholic] Our Lady of Lourdes. Handsome residences line the way, and at the junction, with Bloor street a substantial bridge leads over the ravine into Rosedale, the city's most picturesque suburb.

Bloor is a residential street also, but homes are interspersed with sacred edifices, colleges and schools. On the south side St. Paul's [Anglican] Church, ivied and quaint, may be seen as well as Westminster Presbyterian [now St. Andrew's United], the Bloor Street [Central] Methodist [demolished], the Bloor Street Baptist [near North Street, now Bay, demolished] and, well west on the line, the grey stone walls of the Huron Street [Bloor Street] Presbyterian Church. Moulton Ladies' College [demolished] is on the north side of the street and near it are the residence and lawns of one of the Senators [William McMaster]. West of Yonge street the passenger gets a fine view of Queen's Park, wherein are the University of

Turn-of-the-century penny postcard views along the Belt Line. Above: Spadina Avenue looking north to College Street, Knox College and Belt Line car in the distance. Below: Spadina Avenue near Harbord Street with Belt Line streetcar.

Toronto, whose Norman towers may be seen rising beyond the noble trees, the auxiliary buildings of the University, Wycliffe College and Victoria University as well. The opulent face of McMaster University [now the Royal Conservatory of Music] fronts directly upon Bloor street and west and north of it may be seen the simple substantial walls of one of our millionaires' homes, George Gooderham [now the York Club].

At Spadina avenue, one of the broadest of our thoroughfares, the Belt Line turns south. It makes the circuit of Knox College [now a University of Toronto building] and its grounds before reaching College street, at one corner [northeast] of which is the Broadway Tabernacle of the Methodist faith [demolished]. While the upper portion of Spadina avenue is mainly residential, south of College street it is almost wholly devoted to the business world. As the car turns east into King street a glimpse may be had of Loretto Abbey [southwest Spadina and Wellington], a well-known Catholic seminary, which overlooks the park and fine trees of Clarence Square.

The return run along King street affords a view of Government House, a plain brick structure at the [southwest] corner of Simcoe street, surrounded with well-laid-out gardens, of the old site of Upper Canada College [northwest King and Simcoe], of what was long known as "Macdonnell's Church" [Reverend Daniel James Macdonnell was minister of the church now known as St. Andrew's Presbyterian at the southeast corner of King and Simcoe from its dedication in early 1876 until his death in 1896], of newspaper offices, banks and a miscellany of business buildings. At what was the starting point this passenger may disembark, and if he be a visitor will surely have found good reason for our city's occasional arrogance of the title of Queen.

March 23, 2003

Ma Bell's Birth

What weighs over five pounds, has 2,096 pages, features a cast of many thousands, and has a plot that's impossible to follow? Give up? The latest Bell telephone directory appearing on front porches all over town.

There's quite a contrast between the newest edition and the very first telephone book that was issued in Toronto more than a century ago. Actually, use of the word *book* to describe that first directory is really a misnomer; it was more like a small booklet. The firm that published it was the fledgling Telephone Despatch Company, a local enterprise that provided a pioneer telephone service in the young city using Alexander Graham Bell's recently patented invention. The founders of this new company, which had been incorporated in 1878 with a total investment of $3,000, were optician Charles Potter, Dr. A.M. Rosebrough and brother Melville, and Hugh Neilson. The last gentleman, who lived at 321 Carlton Street, served as the manager of the nascent organization. The company operated on a 24-hour basis and had a total of three employees.

Its first "List of Subscribers" was issued on May 1, 1879, and was printed by Bingham and Taylor, Leader Lane (the small street that still exists on the east side of the King Edward Hotel). This document was, in fact, a three-inch-by-five-inch, four-page cardboard folder containing the names of its 56 customers, a number that included the four founders.

Some of the other Toronto businesses that tried out the new service were commission merchants Chapman and Sons, 91 Front Street East; druggist H.J. Rose, whose store was at the Yonge and Queen intersection; Robert Walker's dry goods store at 35 King Street East (site of today's King Edward Hotel); the offices of the *Globe* and *Telegram* newspapers; the St. Charles Restaurant on lower Yonge Street; and a couple of railway offices (specifically, the Grand Trunk and the Union Pacific). The very first commercial contract was signed between the Toronto Telephone Despatch Company and Messrs. McGaw and Winnett, proprietors of the province's busiest hotel, the Queen's, a rambling structure that stood where the Royal York Hotel is located today.

The majority of these early subscribers were connected via party lines, with six to eight customers on each circuit. No doubt an annoyance, but one that would eventually be phased out once technology caught up with the dreams of the young telephone company.

The Queen's Hotel on Front Street West had Toronto's first commercial telephone.

The first "private" telephone line connected Oliver Mowat's law office on Church Court with the premier's office in the old Parliament Buildings (above) on Front Street, west of Simcoe. (Photo: Ontario Archives)

The first private line connected Oliver Mowat's law office at 24 Church Court with his office in the Parliament Buildings on the north side of Front, just west of Simcoe. The telephone must have been a welcome addition for the very busy Mowat who, as a Father of Confederation, had helped create a new Dominion some years earlier and now served as Ontario's premier and attorney general while still practising law.

The Despatch Company's "List of Subscribers" included the names and addresses of the 56 subscribers, but there were no phone numbers yet, the connection being done manually through an operator at a switchboard. The list also included the protocol to be followed when making or receiving a call: "To converse with subscribers call the Central Office, tell them whom you wish to converse with; as soon as the person desired has answered the operator will connect the two circuits and say 'All Right.' Then the person who called should commence the conversation while the other listens. In each case allow the person calling you to commence the conversation, first giving the subscriber's name. Speak slowly and distinctly, with some force, but not in a high voice; and let the telephone rest against the upper lip. At all times give your hearers time to transfer the telephone to their ear before you speak and be certain a sentence is finished before you reply."

In those far-off days one could not talk and listen at the same time. It was a one-way conversation.

In April 1881 the newly organized Bell Telephone Company of Canada absorbed the pioneer firm and kept Neilson as the manager who ran things in the new Bell office at 10 King Street East.

As more and more people opted for a telephone, the manual system became obsolete and exchanges were introduced. First came MAin, followed by others such as NOrth, JUnction, and BEach. Callers now had to remember two letters and four numbers when placing calls. The introduction of "automatics" came in July 1924 when GRover became the first "dial" exchange. Others quickly followed: ELgin, HOward, HArgrave, et cetera. In 1951 Bell introduced two-letter, five-number dialling (ELgin 1234 became EMpire-4-1234). A decade later ANC (All-Number Calling) was introduced, and soon all the fondly remembered prefix names were gone, replaced by numbers (EMpire-4-1234 became 364-1234). Recently, the addition of the area code became mandatory, resulting in 10-digit numbers.

March 30, 2003

On the Tube

S tretching 4.6 miles from the southern terminus at Union Station northward to Eglinton Avenue, with 10 stations in between, Toronto's first subway line opened in 1954. It came as a welcome relief for many of the city's 700,000 citizens who had often suffered excruciatingly long waits for the lumbering surface streetcars. Today Toronto has a trio of subway lines, totalling 23.9 miles in length and serving 69 stations.

Interestingly, the need for some sort of rapid transit on, over, or under the city's main street was recognized in the early years of the 20th century. First, there was talk of an elevated railway, followed in 1910 by a proposal for a "tube" (a turn-of-the-century term for subway). This latter idea was even put forward on the 1912 civic election ballot. Championed by mayoral candidate Controller Horatio Hocken (Hocken Avenue), the plan had "tubes" operating under Bay and Terauley streets (the latter the extension of Bay north of Queen), then northeast under what is now Ramsden Park to continue north under Yonge to a terminal at St. Clair Avenue. Both Mr. Hocken and his imaginative, if premature, "tube" proposal were defeated. In a strange twist of municipal job shuffling, the far-sighted Hocken would serve as chief magistrate, anyway, when the man who actually won the job as mayor (Reginald Geary, Geary Avenue) decided mid-term that he would prefer the position of city solicitor. Hocken was appointed mayor for the remainder of 1912 and then formally elected by the people to serve again in 1913.

The Yonge Street subway proposal then lay dormant for almost two decades until the malaise of the Great Depression prompted a series of ideas to get men back to work. One of these ideas involved the construction of what was called a "streetcar subway." This concept would see 3,000 men dig a 20-foot-wide trench down the middle of Yonge Street at the bottom of which track would be laid over which ordinary streetcars would operate. Bridges would carry cross streets over the trench while pedestrians would be accommodated on street-level sidewalks on either side of the trench. Needless to say, nothing ever came of this plan.

Under the watchful eye of TTC Inspector Findlay McLeod, Chairman William McBrien takes the controls of the first Yonge subway train on March 30, 1954. McBrien passed away less than three months after this photo was taken. (*Telegram* photo from the *Toronto Sun* Archives)

With the outbreak of the Second World War in 1939, Canadians put other things out of their collective minds and quickly rushed to help England. Suddenly, there were more important issues than solving the Yonge Street traffic problem. Nevertheless, the Toronto Transportation Commission (later renamed the Toronto Transit Commission) was convinced that downtown traffic congestion would become a major problem in postwar Toronto. In addition to ensuring efficient day-to-day operations at this crucial period in the nation's history, TTC officials and staff continued to seek possible solutions to the inevitable transit problems facing Toronto in the future.

An obvious solution was to free up Yonge Street by removing the streetcars and building that elusive subway. One of the most enthusiastic subway advocates was William

The TTC's McBrien Building looms over one of the original Yonge subway trains. Today two of the cars are on view at the Halton County Radial Railway Museum near Rockwood, Ontario. See *www.hcrr.org.* (Courtesy Ted Wickson & JBC Visuals)

Carson McBrien, the chairman of the Toronto Transportation Commission. McBrien, who was born on a farm near Orangeville, Ontario, in 1899, came to Toronto with his family in 1902 and attended Gladstone (now Alexander Muir) and Dovercourt public schools.

One of McBrien's first jobs was that of "call boy" on the floor of the Toronto Stock Exchange. A few years later, having amassed cash assets of $125, he and an older brother opened a hardware store on Bloor Street West. Then, when war was declared on Germany and its allies in 1914, McBrien, like thousands of other young Canadians, joined up and served as a lieutenant in the 95th Battalion and later (and rather fittingly as it would turn out) as a major with the 10th Battalion Canadian Railway Troops. Returning after the war, McBrien served his city first as a member of the Board of Education and then from 1926 to 1929 as a Toronto Harbour commissioner. In 1930 McBrien's municipal and military experience resulted in City Council appointing the young man as a commissioner of the nine-year-old Toronto Transportation Commission. Three years later McBrien was appointed chairman, an influential position that allowed him to pursue his dream of a Yonge Street subway with additional vigour.

McBrien's dream began to take shape officially on September 8, 1949, when work commenced at the Yonge and Wellington intersection.

Exactly four years, six months, and 25 days later Toronto's first subway opened. In the interim, however, McBrien became terminally ill. Nevertheless, he had the tenacity not only to attend the inaugural ceremonies but to help drive the first train out of the new Davisville station. Less than three months later William Carson McBrien was dead.

In 1958, to honour this remarkable Torontonian, the TTC's new head office situated over the Davisville station at Yonge Street and Chaplin Crescent was officially named the McBrien Building.

April 6, 2003

Looking Forward

On the moonless evening of October 9, 1915, 22-year-old Lieutenant Edwin Albert Baker, a member of the 6th Field Company, Royal Canadian Engineers, peered into the darkness in an attempt to get his bearings. He knew he was somewhere near the small Belgian village of Kemmel. He also knew he wasn't far from the enemy's front line. Suddenly, a star shell roared into the inky black sky, illuminating the surrounding landscape with a ghostly white light. A split second later a single shot rang out.

Baker heard a hissing sound, then felt a sharp pain that burned across the top of his face. Instinctively, he raised his hands in a delayed protective reaction only to discover that an enemy bullet had struck him in the left eye, crashing through the upper part of his nose to exit near his right eye. Now it wasn't just the darkness of that cold October night that obscured his vision. The young lieutenant had been blinded, something that by war's end would befall more than 300 other Canadians fighting in what was described as "the war to end all wars."

For Lieutenant Eddy Baker his war was over. After initial treatment at the forward base hospital in Camiers, France, he was transferred to the Second General Hospital, the prewar St. Mark's Ladies' College on the Thames Embankment in south London. Then it was on to St. Dunstan's Hostel, a facility for the blind that had been established by Arthur Pearson, a successful newspaper man whose collection of papers would grow to include several of Great Britain's most prestigious publications, including the *Daily Express* and *Evening Standard*.

There was no doubt that the future had changed totally for the young man who, until that fateful night in October at least, had his eyes set on a career in engineering. Remarkably, Baker's physical loss was to result in an immeasurable gain for the thousands who either were or would become sightless or sight-impaired.

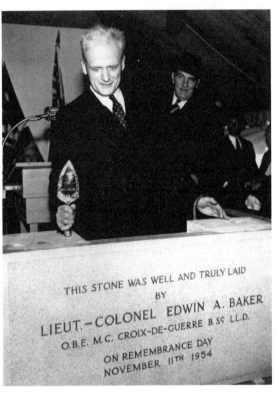

THIS STONE WAS WELL AND TRULY LAID
BY
LIEUT.-COLONEL EDWIN A. BAKER
O.B.E. M.C. CROIX-DE-GUERRE B.SC LL.D.
ON REMEMBRANCE DAY
NOVEMBER 11TH 1954

Edwin Albert Baker taps the cornerstone of the new CNIB Headquarters on Bayview Avenue into place on November 11, 1954.

When Baker returned home, he was appalled at the provisions, or lack thereof, that had been made for the sightless Canadian veterans of the Great War. Baker's tenacity to right this wrong ultimately led to the establishment of the Canadian National Institute for the Blind, an organization that was patterned largely on St. Dunstan's, with which he had a great affinity, and Britain's National Institute for the Blind.

Officially, the CNIB came into existence on March 30, 1918, with Eddie Baker appointed vice-president. A year later the organization moved into its new headquarters, an ancient house that earlier had been the residence of the Honourable George Brown, a Father of Confederation and founder of the *Globe* newspaper. The historic house on St. George Street is now held in trust for the citizens of Ontario by the Ontario Heritage Foundation.

The CNIB remained at Pearson Hall (so named in honour of Baker's long-time friend and mentor) for many years, and even though several structural additions were made to the old building and space was rented in six other Toronto-area buildings, it soon became obvious that what had evolved over the years into a busy organization with nationwide responsibilities now needed to consolidate its activities, hopefully in a modern new headquarters.

A 15-acre site, part of the former "Divadale" estate of the mysterious Colonel Flanagan (it's reported that Diva was his wife's first name) and located just south of the new Sunnybrook Military Hospital on north Bayview Avenue, was selected, despite its remoteness from the city, which caused some initial concern.

As for the funds to build the CNIB's new headquarters, Baker sought out his old friend Lewis Miller Wood, a successful financier who had always been there in the past when the CNIB ran into money problems. Together the two were able to convince D.W. Ambridge, president of Abitibi Power and Paper Company, to head up a fund-raising team that quickly amassed over $3 million for the new facility.

The cornerstone of what would be called Bakerwood (in honour of the indefatigable Eddie Baker and his pal Lew) was tapped into place by Lieutenant Colonel Edwin A. Baker, OBE, MC, Croix-de-Guerre,

The wrecker's hoarding surrounds Bakerwood as demolition of the old CNIB building is about to begin in March 2003.

on Remembrance Day 1954. The new building was officially opened on April 16, 1956, by Vincent Massey, the governor general of the day.

Incidentally, the location of this sparkling new headquarters high above what had become, in the short span of time since the site was originally selected, a busy traffic artery would certainly present a problem for its many visually challenged visitors. The answer was either traffic lights or an overhead pedestrian bridge. As far as the Toronto and York Roads Commission was concerned, traffic lights were out of the question. That left the bridge. But there was no money to build it. This time it was the Atkinson Foundation to the rescue, with $60,000 for the bridge (of special design, fixed at one end, and movable at the other to allow for expansion and contraction) plus a similar amount to furnish the new building's library and auditorium.

April 13, 2003

* Pearson Hall on St. George Street served the CNIB well for 37 years, Bakerwood for another 47. Nevertheless, demolition of the 1956 headquarters was completed in 2003, and a newer building, funded primarily through the sale of 12 acres of the original CNIB property, officially opened on Bayview Avenue in June 2005. It's barrier-free in its design and serves as the CNIB's national and Ontario divisions and Toronto District Office. There's also been an expansion of one of the organization's most popular features — its library.

The Big, Big Smoke

On April 20, 1904, thousands of disbelieving Torontonians, having heard rumours that the very heart of their beloved city of 226,365 souls had been destroyed by fire, quietly made their way downtown, fearful of what they would find. In an era well before the advent of radio, television, or Internet reporting, citizens had to rely on the local newspaper (and most of those stories were hours or days old), word of mouth from neighbours, or stories relayed over the telephone for updates on events unfolding around them. Without confirmation through one of these methods, no sane person could ever believe that such a conflagration had destroyed the city's commercial heart. They had to see it for themselves.

Approaching the business area south of King and west of Yonge streets, Torontonians encountered a view that was truly unbelievable. Virtually every building on Bay, Wellington, and Front streets, right down to the warehouses and docks at the water's edge, had been visited by the "fire fiend," with most succumbing to the roaring flames. The once-busy streets and sidewalks were littered with fallen brick, while thick acrid smoke and the smell of charred wood filled the air. This wasn't Toronto; it was Hell.

Subsequent insurance company and fire department investigations placed the number of destroyed or severely damaged buildings at almost 125, with monetary losses in excess of $10 million. Worse still,

6,000 people were out of work. Could Toronto survive this setback? Many believed it wouldn't be long before Toronto's rival at the head of the lake, Hamilton, would assume the role of new commercial heart of the province.

Bay Street looking north from Wellington towards City Hall, 1904.

Front Street looking west across Yonge, Bank of Montreal (now the Hockey Hall of Fame) on the right, 1904.

Those same investigations traced the source of the fire to the Currie Neckwear Company factory on the north side of Wellington Street a few doors west of the Bay Street corner. Up on the top floor a hot iron had been left too close to a pile of rags. Soon after the City Hall clock had chimed 8:00 p.m. that cold, blustery April 19 evening, flames erupted and quickly blew out nearby windows. Seeking fresh air, the flames leaped out of those windows and, caught by the wind, swept into adjacent buildings. Soon all four buildings at the Bay and Wellington corner were in flames.

And the fire just kept spreading. Low water pressure in the mains (a problem that City Council had refused to correct, even though downtown Toronto had been visited by a trio of major conflagrations over the previous decade) meant that the task facing the firefighters was an almost impossible one. They would do their best, but just how far the flames would spread was anybody's guess. As the fire grew in

Firemen and equipment in use at the time of the Great Toronto Fire of 1904.

intensity and more buildings came crashing down, it was obvious the city could use some help. Calls went out, and soon firemen and equipment began arriving on railway flatcars from Hamilton, Brantford, Niagara Falls, and Buffalo. Even the nearby communities of Kew Beach, Toronto Junction, and East Toronto (all still autonomous entities), as small as they were, came to the big city's assistance.

The fire was finally declared "under control" nine hours after the first alarm was rung. While no one was killed as a direct result of what would become known as the Great Toronto Fire of 1904, several firefighters were badly injured. A fatality attributable to massive clean-up operations that followed the fire did occur some days later when young John Croft, a recent immigrant from England, was killed attempting to knock down a building's walls using dynamite.

April 20, 2003

Defending the Empire

One of the most imposing war memorials in Toronto is the one located in the University Avenue median just north of the Queen Street corner. As the inscription on the granite base states, the monument was erected "To the memory and in honour of the Canadians who died defending the Empire in the South African War, 1899–1902." The expression "defending the Empire" described the way most, but not all, Canadians saw the conflict that pitted the locals (Boers) living in the South African states of the Transvaal and Orange Free State against the military might of the British Empire. War was declared on October 12, 1899, with hostilities ending on May 31, 1902. During that period, more than 8,000 Canadians volunteered to aid the Mother Country. Of that number, four were awarded the Victoria Cross. More than 240 never returned and rest permanently in various cemeteries throughout what is now the Republic of South Africa. In contrast, the British lost over 5,000, the Boers approximately 3,700. Amazingly, more than half of all deaths were disease-related.

The idea of a memorial to the Canadian dead seems to have been, for whatever reason or reasons, a tough sell. Money was slow in arriving, resulting in the war being over for almost eight years before the cornerstone of Toronto sculptor Walter Allward's imposing design was finally tapped into place. (Allward has a number of other works in Toronto

Dignitaries pose for the photographer as the new South African War Memorial is officially unveiled on May 24, 1910. The trio of gentlemen in front includes Sir John French (plumed hat), Ontario Lieutenant Governor John Gibson, and Premier Sir John Whitney.

Where is it? Looking north on University at Queen, 1960. Work on the new subway forced the disassembly and storage of the monument. It was returned and re-assembled once work at the corner had been completed.

but is probably best known for his magnificent Vimy Memorial in France, which was unveiled by King Edward VIII in 1936.)

A little more than eight months after work commenced on the new South African War Memorial a special ceremony was held during which Sir John French, commander of all British cavalry operations during the war, did the honours. The year following French's brief visit to Toronto he was appointed chief of staff of the British army.

Listed on the memorial are battles in which Canadians participated. At the bottom of the memorial is a trio of figures, the centre one representing Canada. Beside her are representations of a cavalry soldier and a member of the infantry. The winged figure atop the 65-foot-high column represents Victorious Peace. A newspaper report describing the event stated that there were plans to affix a bronze plaque listing the names of all the war dead on the back of the soaring shaft. For some reason (money?) that plaque never materialized.

May 4, 2003

A Century of Grandeur

On May 11, 1903, Toronto financier, businessman, and philanthropist George Gooderham walked into the lobby of the new King Edward Hotel on King Street East and saw that all was good. Finally, his new $2-million hotel was ready to serve the world, at least those who were planning to come to Toronto. Incidentally, Gooderham didn't have to sign the hotel guestbook set in plain view on the countertop of the main desk. As a director of the Toronto Hotel Company, he and his fellow directors had done that the day before to ensure they would be first in the book. Out of curiosity, however, Gooderham inspected the register and discovered that John A. Davidson of Chicago, whose company had supplied the hotel's marble work, was his first paying guest.

The idea of a sumptuous new hotel to serve the needs of well-heeled visitors to the fast-growing city as well as the city's elite, a hotel that would feature well-appointed meeting rooms, magnificent dining rooms, and ballrooms where visitors could dance the night away, had been on Gooderham's mind for a long time. Not only would it be good for the city, but in the proper location such an amenity would help preserve the value of his numerous real-estate holdings, the majority of which were located east of the city's main street, Yonge. Gooderham witnessed the trend being followed by many of the new businesses to seek property west of Yonge, over on Bay and even York streets. Gooderham would do whatever he deemed necessary to ensure that the

Early conceptual sketch of the new King Edward Hotel, circa 1900.

area east of Yonge would continue to be the business and financial centre of Toronto, just as it had been from the city's start. A key component of his plan would be the construction of a magnificent new hotel.

The idea had first been discussed by Gooderham and a few of his wealthy friends in the late 1890s. In fact, preliminary drawings of the new "Palace Hotel" had somehow appeared in the city newspapers. The property secured by the promoters on which the new building would be erected was the site of Robert Walker's Golden Lion store. The businessmen had also convinced City Council to extend Victoria Street south of King (where it ended) to connect with Scott Street. This was key to the development of the new project in that it now gave the hotel extra frontage that could be developed. However, an extension on the south side of Colborne Street, which would be accessed via a bridge over Colborne, was never approved. Years later the hotel did expand by erecting a new 450-room, 18-floor addition east of and adjoining the original structure.

Almost coincident with work beginning on the "Palace," Queen Victoria passed away. In honour of her successor, and son, a new name for the hotel was thrown out for discussion. The Edward VII Hotel had a nice ring, but before long it was modified to the current King Edward Hotel.

May 11, 2003

Riding the Rails

On May 16, 1853, the first scheduled passenger train in what is now the Province of Ontario left a diminutive wooden station not far from the corner of today's busy Front and Bay streets on its way northwards to a place called Matchell's Corners, a small community on the western outskirts of Aurora. But Matchell's would be the northern terminus for only a short time. Within the month passenger rail service was being provided all the way to Bradford. Stops along the route included Davenport, Thornhill, Richmond Hill, King, Matchell's, and Newmarket. Providing the motive power for that first quartet of passenger cars was an engine called, appropriately enough, *Toronto*, a recent product of the James Good Foundry, located on the east side of Yonge Street just steps north of Queen Street (about where the Elgin and Winter Garden Theatre Centre stands today).

The idea behind this pioneer railway line can be traced back to a meeting held in Toronto in the late summer of 1834, the year the city was incorporated and just seven years after the first train began operating south of the border. At this meeting a small group of entrepreneurs wrestled with the idea of building either a railway or canal to connect the city of 9,254 souls on the north shore of Lake Ontario with Lake Simcoe. There was no doubt that bringing the riches of the north to the city quickly and at a low cost would soon make the investors wealthy men.

The *Toronto* hauled the first scheduled passenger train service out of the City of Toronto on May 16, 1853.

One of the stations along the way to Matchell's Corners was Davenport, located just west of today's busy St. Clair Avenue and Caledonia Road intersection.

However, the time wasn't right and the plans soon faded only to be revived 15 years later by another group, this time operating under the grandiose title of the Toronto, Simcoe, and Lake Huron Union Railroad Company. The Lake Huron part of the title reflected the company's high hopes to provide a direct rail connection with Michigan. To raise the money necessary to build the line, one of the prime investors in the project, Frederick Chase Capreol, suggested collecting funds through a general lottery with stock in the project as prizes. This concept never caught on with the public, and soon more conventional sources of capital were sought and eventually secured.

Work on the new railway finally began on October 15, 1851, and less than two years later cheering crowds lined the route as *Toronto* and its four passenger cars chugged into history. In 1858 the Ontario, Simcoe, and Huron (to its detractors, the Oats, Straw, and Hay) became the Northern Railway of Canada, later the Northern and Northwestern, which was absorbed into the Grand Trunk which, in turn, became part of Canadian National Railways.

May 18, 2003

West's Side Story

I 've said it before and I'll say it again — one of the nicest things about writing this column and contributing a short Toronto history feature to radio station AM740 is meeting my readers and listeners. And every once in a while those meetings result in uncovering material that's perfect for a column. A recent conversation with Mr. Albert West is a case in point. He initially called to say that he had in his possession a few of the photographs his father had taken many years ago and was I interested in seeing them.

Was I? I sure was, and it wasn't long before I was at the Wests' front door.

Before I describe some of those old photos Mr. West revealed, permit me to share a few details about the photographer himself. Albert's father, Ernest, was only 12 when *his* father immigrated with the family to Toronto from England. They settled in a small house on Maitland Street in the Yonge-College-Carlton area. At that time Toronto's population stood at 120,000 or so, and the Town of Parkdale had only recently been annexed, as had a thousand or so acres on the east side of the Don River at a place called Riverdale. The mayor was William Holmes Howland, whose two-year term as chief magistrate was beset with a major scandal, not over computer-leasing as has been the case recently, but by unscrupulous city officials who were involved in dastardly schemes to inflate the price of coal, the prime source of heat for most of the city's houses.

Melinda Street looking east from near Bay Street. Ernest West's photo of the devastating Osgoodby fire, January 10, 1895. (Photo courtesy Albert West)

As a young man, Ernest worked in the drugstore of a Mr. Petrie on Avenue Road north of Bloor and later as a manufacturing chemist with the A.B. Shuttleworth Company on Wilton (now Dundas) Street. Ernest soon developed a keen interest in all aspects of a new hobby sweeping the continent — photography. It was a few of the negatives and prints from his father's collection that Albert West wanted me to see.

Of particular interest were several four-inch-by-five-inch glass plate negatives that were in a small box marked "Toronto fire, 1904." Prints made of these negatives, however, showed a row of burned-out buildings with a few names still visible that simply didn't match the listings in my directories describing the city in that year. In fact, it soon became obvious that the fire captured in those views wasn't the one that occurred in April 1904, destroying more than 120 buildings and inflicting more than $10 million in damages on the city.

At first I was unable to make any sense of the images. Then I remembered seeing a building similar to the one in the photo in a sketch that appeared in volume 2 of *Robertson's Landmarks of Toronto* (a six-volume set of books containing hundreds of history-related articles that appeared in J. Ross Robertson's *Evening Telegram* newspaper from 1894 to 1914).

Comparing that sketch with Ernest's photograph left no doubt that the young photographer had, in fact, captured the ruins of the Osgoodby Building fire that had devastated nearly a dozen nearby buildings north and east of the Bay and Wellington street intersection on the evening of January 10, 1895. The total monetary damage was in excess of $700,000. It was in the Osgoodby Building, where the fire had started and a building that stood about where the courtyard of Commerce Court is today, that William Osgoodby published, or should I say, had published his weekly magazine, *The Times*.

Photographer Ernest West. (Photo courtesy Albert West)

While not as serious as the Great Fire of 1904, the Osgoodby conflagration was important in that it was the second in a series of three extremely damaging fires that ravaged the city's downtown core in little more than two months in early 1895.

The first (January 6, 1895) was the *Globe* Building fire that devastated several structures in and around the Yonge and Melinda Street corner, including the five-year-old building in which the *Globe* was published. Toronto Fire Chief Richard Ardagh suffered severe injuries during this fire that were to contribute to his death three weeks later.

That fire was followed four days later by the Osgoodby blaze that was followed exactly two months later by the loss of Robert Simpson's large department store at the southwest corner of Yonge and Queen. (The building that replaced this structure still stands on the corner as the Hudson's Bay store.) Many other businesses were also obliterated in the Simpson's fire, with serious damages

Artist's sketch in the January 11, 1895, edition of the *Evening Telegram* that helped identify Ernest West's photograph.

inflicted on Knox Presbyterian Church on Richmond Street west of Yonge. Several years later the congregation moved to a beautiful new church on Spadina, just south of Harbord.

Interestingly, each fire did approximately $700,000 worth of damage. Politicians and citizens alike had a field day demanding that more modern fire equipment be purchased and that a new high-pressure water system be installed immediately. Nothing happened. Nine years later the city nearly burned to the ground.

Special thanks to Albert West for sharing his dad's photo with me and my readers.

May 25, 2003

Sporty Venue

I call the new Ricoh Coliseum down at Toronto's Canadian National Exhibition Grounds "new," but the building itself was first known by the rather grand title of Royal Coliseum and was built as the home of the newly established Royal Agricultural Winter Fair. However, in its early years the Coliseum was also identified as either the Civic Arena or Live Stock Arena.

The Ricoh Coliseum (Ricoh being the copier, camera, and electronics people) sports more than a "few" upgrades. For instance, a new roof has been built, one that's a full 20 feet higher than the old. A new main floor that's five feet lower than the original has also been completed. And new, much more comfortable seating has increased the arena's former 7,500 capacity to 10,000 (11,500 for concerts).

Additionally, the Ricoh Coliseum has a new ice-making plant and associated under-floor piping as well as all the modern-day amenities (heating, cooling, plumbing) and numerous safety features. And the Ricoh has something the old Coliseum never had: 38 private suites suspended from the roof on the east and west sides of the arena. In total nearly $40 million was spent to give the Ricoh Coliseum a new lease on life as a hockey arena, exhibit hall, and concert venue. Interestingly, the original price assigned to the new Coliseum was $1 million. However, by mid-1922 that figure had risen to $1.7 million and probably topped $2 million by the time the building opened officially later that year.

Work progresses on the construction of the new Coliseum at the Canadian National Exhibition Grounds on September 2, 1921.

More than 80 years later the roof is being raised and the floor lowered (with millions of dollars spent on other improvements) to ready the Ricoh Coliseum for its new career as a sports, concert, and exhibition venue.

You know something? I just realized that plans call for the new Ricoh Coliseum to host the first home game of the Roadrunners, Toronto's new team in the American Hockey League. Will they make it? Of course they will!

Well, at least I'm pretty sure they will. Now I don't want to put a whammy on the project, but the original Coliseum got off to a faltering start. Plans were to have the building ready in time for the official opening of the newly established Royal Agricultural Winter Fair, a classy fur-coat-and-tails event that was scheduled for the evening of November 16, 1921.

Unfortunately, a hitch in the installation of the heating system forced the postponement of the first Winter Fair until the following year. (Actually, the officials did consider opening the building without heat but were eventually convinced that the patrons and visitors in fur coats and mink wraps would just be too cold to enjoy themselves.)

By mid-December 1921, work on the new Coliseum was finally completed, and city officials felt that the building should be used for something and not wait until the Winter Fair was ready to go nearly a year later. As a result, the new building actually opened with a school sports tournament. It was also decided that the CNE should go ahead and use the building during the 1922 edition of the exhibition.

And so it was that the people for whom the Coliseum was originally built weren't the first to use it. In fact, the Winter Fair's turn didn't come until November 22, 1922, when Lieutenant Governor Henry Cockshutt officially opened both the Royal Coliseum and the first Royal Agricultural Winter Fair.

June 1, 2003

* The Toronto Roadrunner hockey team lasted but one season. The Ricoh Coliseum is now the home rink of the Toronto Marlies of the American Hockey League.

Taking to the Road

The Toronto Automobile Club, an organization later known as the Ontario Motor League, then Canadian Automobile Association Toronto, and since 1995 CAA Central Ontario, got its start in 1903, not long after the first few wheezing, sputtering "horseless carriages" began appearing on Toronto city streets late in the 19th century. It was nothing formal, mind you, just a group of wealthy businessmen interested in the newest wonder of the age getting together to chat about tillers, spoked wheels, and chain drives.

However, as time went on and automobiles became more frequent users of the highways and byways, it became obvious that their owners, often the target of resentment and jealousy from those who preferred horse power to horsepower, needed to speak with one voice. It was with this in mind that on May 4, 1903, a group of 27 enthusiastic "motorists" (among whom were Sir John Eaton and Dr. Perry Doolittle, who would later become "the father of the Trans-Canada Highway") met at the Queen's Hotel on Front Street West, an ancient hostelry that stood about where the Royal York is today. At that meeting the group formed the Toronto Automobile Club.

The new organization's stated aims were to "develop interest in automobiling in Canada and to assist in the promotion of all that pertains thereto, to assist the movement in favour of better roads, to maintain discipline among members as to the proper speed at which

In this early newspaper ad, Hyslop Brothers, one of Toronto's foremost bicycle dealers, added the new Olds horseless carriage to their stock of transportation devices.

An outing in the family's new "flivver" on a dusty road somewhere north of Toronto.

automobiles should be driven and to co-operate with the legislature in securing fair legislation on this subject."

One of the first things the new organization did was to try to convince provincial lawmakers that the existing speed limit of eight miles per hour was inappropriate. Club members arranged to take the authorities on a demonstration drive to show that driving at 10 miles per hour wasn't "scorching." Their guests agreed and the limit was raised.

From that first membership list of 27, today's CAA Central Ontario boasts more than 1.7-million members.

June 8, 2003

More of Ernest West's Old Photographs

In a previous column I featured an old photograph taken more than a century ago by reader Albert West's father, Ernest. Through a little sleuthing I was able to determine that the image depicted on the brittle glass negative (that now rests in the protective custody of the Toronto Archives) was, in fact, the ruins of the Osgoodby Building that was located on Melinda Street right about where the courtyard at Commerce Court is today. The Osgoodby structure was where the second of a trio of devastating fires erupted on January 6, 1895. Preceded by the *Globe* fire and followed by the Simpson's store conflagration, these three fires laid waste to vast areas of downtown Toronto in little more than two months.

Well, in Albert's collection of old photos there were two others that, in the vernacular of today, just "blew me away." Both are reproduced here. Under a magnifying glass the route and destination signs on the two cars identify each of them as being on the Church Street route. This fact makes the views especially interesting to me (and I would imagine to other streetcar buffs, as well) since that was the first route to be converted from horse-drawn streetcars to the modern new electric cars. Is it possible that Ernest West intentionally snapped these photos to capture this historic event in Toronto transportation history?

While we'll probably never know for sure the exact dates these views were taken, here are a few Toronto streetcar facts we do know.

Ernest West's photo of a Toronto horse-drawn streetcar on Church Street, circa 1892.

Another of Ernest West's photos shows one of the city's new electric streetcars on the Church route sometime in the mid-1890s.

The Church route (from the "old" Union Station west of York Street via Front and Church streets to Bloor both ways) was started as a horse-car line in 1881. The conversion to electric operation took place in August 1892, with the first of the electric cars (for buffs, car number 270) entering service on the 15th of that month. Coincident with the inauguration of electric service on Church, the horse-drawn cars were moved to other routes. The total conversion of the city street railway system was completed a little more than two years later.

Other facts we know are that horse car number 260, a vehicle that was described as a "closed 10-foot car," was built in 1890 by the privately owned Toronto Street Railway Company (TSR) in its car-building shop at the northwest corner of Front and Frederick streets. It was one of the last horse cars to be built in Toronto.

One of the city's first electric streetcars is seen in the second photo. Car number 276 was also built by the TSR in its Front Street shops. It was converted to electric operation following the takeover of the company by the new Toronto Railway Company. The car entered service in September 1892, just weeks after the city's first electric route began on Church Street the previous August 15. Interestingly, this car went on to have a rather diverse life. In 1903 it was converted into a trailer and then, after the devastating forest fire that destroyed much of Haileybury, Ontario, in the fall of 1922, trailer number 276 plus another 84 old streetcars were loaded onto Grand Trunk Railway flatcars and sent north where they served as temporary residences for those citizens of Haileybury who lost their homes in the fire.

June 15, 2003

All About Bob

With all the recent media coverage of comedian Bob Hope and his 100th birthday, I was disappointed but not totally surprised by the lack of attention given to any of Hope's visits north of the border. While it's true he spent hundreds of hours entertaining in various countries and theatres of war all over the globe, it's equally true that he spent many, many hours in Canada, especially in Toronto. In fact, in a Toronto newspaper interview in 1941, Hope confirmed that one of his first stage performances ("I'm pretty sure it was in 1930," he reminisced) was at the city's famous Shea's Hippodrome on the west side of Bay Street, then known as Terauley Street. This grand old theatre was demolished in the mid-1950s to make way for Nathan Phillips Square. If indeed it was in 1930, that would make his visit to Toronto a full seven years before his screen debut in *The Big Broadcast of 1938* (the film was actually released in 1937).

Interestingly, that 1941 interview was done when Hope was back in Toronto promoting his new movie *Caught in the Draft* in which he starred with Dorothy Lamour and Eddie Bracken. While in Toronto he was asked to appear at the opening of the new Strathcona Palace Pier roller rink down on the waterfront.

As an aside, funds for the construction of this attraction that was to be built at the mouth of the Humber River in Etobicoke Township had been raised by simply promising investors that the structure (designed after the Palace Pier in Brighton, England) would quickly become one of the city's top amusement places. It would make those who invested in it very rich. As it turned out, that wasn't the case and what years later would become known as the Palace Pier Dance Hall would sit unused and empty for more than a decade.

The opening that Hope attended in June 1941 featured a five-day roller-skating marathon with all money raised destined for the British War Victims Fund. So even before the United States entered the Second World War, Bob Hope was doing his "bit."

During Bob Hope's 1965 CNE show, someone snapped this picture from the Grandstand's front row.

Hope also became a regular feature at the Canadian National Exhibition's annual Grandstand Shows where he holds the record for most appearances. Between 1957 and 1978 he appeared on the mammoth stage five times. It would have been seven, but CNE officials felt it unwise to have an American, and an ex Englishman at that, headline a Canadian-produced show in Queen Elizabeth II's coronation year.

The Strathcona Palace Pier roller rink at the mouth of the Humber River as it looked when it was opened by radio and movie star Bob Hope in 1941.

Nevertheless, Hope became so popular with Torontonians that in 1976 he was asked to officially open the CNE, which he did before more than 12,000 fans at the Bandshell. It was there that Hope admitted that he had left England, where he was born May 29, 1903, after he realized he couldn't be king. He then went on to tell the crowd that he had an engagement in Washington, D.C., but would return to do the CNE Grandstand show later in the week where he would tell the same jokes but for a different salary.

In addition to many public appearances at the CNE, Maple Leaf Gardens, and the O'Keefe Centre, fans will remember Hope's participation in numerous benefits such as the one that helped raise money for the new Jewish Community Centre on north Bathurst Street.

June 22, 2003

---

* Bob Hope passed away, age 100, on July 27, 2003, not long after this column first appeared.

Before Tim Horton
There Was Downyflake

Hands up, all of you who think Tim Horton invented the doughnut. Well, I guess if you're too young to have memories of a time when the Toronto Maple Leafs hockey team used to win the Stanley Cup on a regular basis, the profusion of Tim Hortons shops (nearly 200 in the Greater Toronto Area alone plus several thousand across Canada and close to 200 more in the United States) might lead the young'uns to believe that Tim Horton was, at the very least, a baker of some note.

But for those of us who grew up in the 1950s and 1960s, we know better. The name Tim Horton wearing sweater number 7 was associated with the Toronto Maple Leafs hockey team from the time he joined as a rookie defenceman in 1952 until he was traded to the New York Rangers after the 1969–1970 season. Tim's name appears on Lord Stanley's cup four times, following Leaf victories in 1962, 1963, 1964, and 1967. (Ah, those were the days!)

Tragically, Horton died on February 21, 1974, as a result of a traffic accident on the Queen Elizabeth Highway. At the time he was a member of the Buffalo Sabres and was returning home after losing a game in Toronto against his old team.

Tim Horton's interest in fast foods actually began while he was still playing hockey when he invested in a not very successful string of hamburger restaurants. He then got the idea of specializing in coffee and doughnuts and opened the first Tim Horton store in downtown

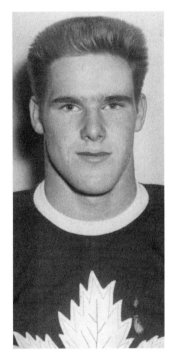

National Hockey League All-Star defenceman Tim Horton (1930–1974).

Hamilton in 1964. Note that it was called Tim Horton and it wasn't until later that the enterprise became Tim Horton's and later still Tim Hortons (with no apostrophe) as it is called today.

The first Toronto-area store, and the 20th in the chain, opened on June 1, 1970, on the Queensway in Etobicoke. It's still at that location, though much modernized.

While Tim Hortons is the predominant coffee-and-doughnut chain in modern-day Toronto, when I was much younger I remember another popular coffee-and-doughnut chain in town. It was called Downyflake Donuts, and the two stores I can recall were down at Sunnyside and near the northwest corner of the Bathurst and Bloor intersection, not far from the Alhambra Theatre and just up the street from our place at 758 Bathurst Street, phone number MElrose 2154.

(By the way, those last two items were the most important facts in my young memory bank. I was told by my parents that if I ever got lost, simply give those important facts to a policeman and he'd get me home.)

The popular Downyflake doughnut shop on the north side of Lake Shore Boulevard West opposite Sunnyside Amusement Park, circa 1950.

The Optimist's Creed was proudly displayed in all Downyflake restaurants. As true today as it was back then.

Unfortunately, other than recalling a marvellous doughnut-making machine in the store window and a copy of the most important piece of poetry ever penned on the wall (a work I tried unsuccessfully to incorporate into the required poetry memorization program in Miss Bealey's English class at North Toronto Collegiate), I'm afraid I don't know much about the company itself. I'd appreciate hearing from any reader who might be able to fill me in on the history of the Downyflake organization.

July 6, 2003

Symbol of Early Days

While the decrease in attendance at most of our tourist attractions is a serious matter, there is a definite upside to this downturn. With the smaller crowds in town, now is the perfect time for local people to get out and discover Toronto. After all, there must be some reason why over the years Toronto has been (and will again be) such a popular destination.

Here's a for-instance. When was the last time that you, or your family or your friends, visited Black Creek Pioneer Village? Located at the southeast corner of Jane Street and Steeles Avenue West, the village boasts some three dozen or so old buildings, some totally unique in their architectural style, many home to professions not seen in decades, but all symbolic of an earlier Ontario. As progress overran the little villages and towns throughout Southern Ontario, each of these "orphans" was deemed "in the way," and it was only the move to Black Creek Pioneer Village that saved these structures from total annihilation.

The idea of a "pioneer village" was first discussed shortly after Hurricane Hazel roared through Ontario in mid-October 1954. Many areas adjacent to the Humber River, including Black Creek itself, were flooded. The death toll approached 100, while property losses were in the millions of dollars.

In an attempt to ensure that such destruction wouldn't happen in the future, officials of the Humber Valley Conservation Authority (now part of the Toronto and Region Conservation Authority) expropriated

Half Way House as it looked in its original location at the northwest corner of Kingston Road and Midland Avenue in the Township of Scarborough, circa 1920.

Half Way House today, preserved and experiencing a new life at Toronto's Black Creek Pioneer Village.

flood-prone areas, including land along Black Creek in the northwest quadrant of the newly formed Municipality of Metropolitan Toronto. It was on part of this property that a village consisting of pre-1867 structures would be developed.

Interestingly, the first few structures to be preserved in what would eventually become Black Creek Pioneer Village were those of the pioneer Stong family who had settled the land on which the village would grow in the early 1800s. The Stong grain barn, piggery, smokehouse, and butchery, as well as the family's first and second houses (erected in 1816 and 1832 respectively), make up the heart of today's village. Other structures on the site include the Laskay General Store (a thriving business that was moved from the tiny community of Laskay, not far from the current King Road/Highway 400 interchange), the circa 1830 Doctor's House (moved to the village from Brampton), the 1858 Wilmot Township Town Hall (Wilmot is near Waterloo), and the circa 1830 Mackenzie House. The last resident of this log structure, which was originally located in Woodbridge, was Major Alexander "Lex" Mackenzie, an area legend who has been immortalized in the name of Major Mackenzie Drive north of the city.

Of particular interest, especially to people who live in the southern part of Scarborough, is Half Way House. Originally located at the northwest corner of the busy Kingston Road–Midland Avenue intersection, this former inn was built in 1849 and was so named because it stood approximately halfway between the farming community in and around Dunbarton (near today's White's Road and Highway 2 in Pickering) and Toronto's St. Lawrence Market at the corner of Jarvis and Front streets. The land on which the inn stood was part of a Crown Grant given to Sarah Ashbridge in 1799. This is the same Sarah Ashbridge, the pioneer Toronto family matriarch whose name is remembered in the Ontario Heritage Foundation's Ashbridge House on Queen Street East.

Half Way House was saved from demolition in the mid-1960s when the Metropolitan Toronto and Region Conservation Authority bought it for $1,000 and spent another $12,000 to have it moved from its original site to the village. After its restoration as a 1967 centennial project, the building, in addition to being a fine example of a typical Ontario wayside inn and stagecoach stop, became a restaurant that serves delicious and hearty meals. In fact, the setting is such that you can almost hear your stagecoach approach.

July 13, 2003

How We Envisioned It

Just when I think I'm going to have trouble coming up with a subject for the next "The Way We Were" column, up pops another idea. And while many of my stories deal strictly with the past, often an idea has some connection with a present-day news story.

Take the recent announcement by officials of Fairmont Hotels and Resorts, Inc., that in the not too distant future, the landmark Royal York sign atop Toronto's famous downtown hotel will disappear and in its place there will be a new sign that simply identifies the place as the Fairmont. This new sign, in keeping with similar signs on other company properties, was to make no reference to the name of the hotel on which it has been erected. As it would turn out, the report that the words *Royal York* would be removed was incorrect. But the very idea stirred up a real hornet's nest.

Actually, the story of how the hotel got the name Royal York in the first place is an interesting one. Rumours of a new, yet unnamed 1,000-room, $8-million hotel first surfaced and were reported in Toronto's *Telegram* newspaper of November 26, 1926. While the developer wasn't named, the location of the new structure was identified as Front Street West with a tunnel connection to the new Union Station then under construction. It wasn't difficult to deduce that the site would have to be the one occupied by the ancient Queen's Hotel whose demolition had been rumoured for months. Approximately six months later another story appeared, this time detailing the land the

developer, now identified as Canadian Pacific Railway, had acquired and indeed much of it included the old Queen's. However, the new name was still unknown; it was simply the CPR Hotel.

It wasn't long, however, before E.W. Beatty, chairman of the board of the Canadian Pacific Hotel Association, let the cat out of the bag when he announced the new hotel would be known as the Royal York. In discussing the choice of this name, Beatty referred to the day in August 1793 (August 27, to be precise) when the newly established province's first lieutenant governor, John Graves Simcoe, called his new town site "our Royal Town of York." In this case the word *York* referred to the title of Frederick, Duke of York, the second eldest son of the reigning monarch, King George III.

While the hotel was known as the Royal York from the day it opened on June 11, 1929, the large sign atop the building didn't appear until August 1960. The block-letter version was altered to script letters a couple of decades later. By the way, that proposed cost of $8 million in the 1926 press release mushroomed to $20 million by the time the place opened two years later.

So what's a few more dollars to expand that proposed new sign from the Fairmont to the Fairmont Royal York. I'd like to think that minor alteration would please everyone.

And that's exactly what happened.

July 20, 2003

Look on the Sunnyside

Of all the subjects I write about, the one that generates the most feedback concerns stories that feature any aspect of the old Sunnyside Amusement Park. In fact, a recent column about little Downyflake Donuts on the north side of Lake Shore Boulevard, a short distance west of the park's popular merry-go-rounds (interestingly, the horses from one of them still twirl at Disneyland in California) generated enough material for several more columns. Now all I need are some details about owners Lou Epstein and Bud Porter as well as a few more pictures of the little restaurant to go along with those stories. Can anybody help?

It wasn't until after the Downyflake story ran that I suddenly realized some of my more youthful readers, as well as many newcomers to Toronto, probably have no idea what this city treasure from the past was all about and where it was located. Permit me to rectify that oversight and offer an interesting fact about the name Sunnyside itself that I only recently came across.

Sunnyside Amusement Park was the creation of the Toronto Harbour Commission (now known as the Toronto Port Authority), an organization that was established by the federal government in 1911 to bring some order to the chaos that over the years had befallen Toronto's waterfront. The commission's area of responsibility started at the foot of Victoria Park Avenue to the east and took in all the waterfront properties

A. R. ROCHE,
Wellington-st.
Toronto, July 6, 1860.
Tr963-1t 676-1t

FOR SALE,
AND IMMEDIATE POSSESSION
GIVEN,
That Beautiful Suburban Villa,
KNOWN AS
SUNNYSIDE !

SITUATE on the north bank of Lake Ontario, within 100 yards of the Lake

The Great Western Railway passes in front without having to be crossed from the city side. The Entrance Hall is 23 feet by 16 feet ; an octagonal Drawing Room, 24 feet by 24 feet , Parlour, 20 feet by 16 feet ; Dining Room, 24 feet by 18 feet , Butler's Pantry, large Kitchen and Scullery, seven Bed Rooms, Bath Room, and a Verandah around the south front, 100 feet long, large Wine and Beer Cellars, Coach House and stabling for eight horses, Harness Rooms, Coachman's and Gardener's Rooms, Ice House and Larder of the best description, Cow and Fowl Houses, fitted up with every convenience. A large Kitchen Garden and

Beautiful Ornamental Park-like Grounds,
COMPRISING ABOUT NINE ACRES,

Round the house. Also, EIGHT ACRES OF BUSH LAND.

If required, 25 acres more, with a beautiful creek meandering through it, could be obtained.

The above property is a mile and a half west of the city limits, consequently the taxes are merely nominal. It is well adapted for a gentleman of large family, having sons to educate, from its proximity to Upper Canada College, the different Universities, law Society, &c., &c., &c.

Or any enterprising man, with some means,who understands keeping a summer boarding house, would find this a good opening, for since the proprietor, Geo. H. Cheney, Esq., left it, it has been visited by thousands in Pic Nic Parties ; and not unfrequently His Excellency Sir Edmund Head, his lady and suite, have been of these parties.

The above property is well worthy the attention of any one having a small capital to invest, as the Assignees must sell to wind up the estate.

For further particulars enquire of JOHN G. HOWARD, Esq., Colborne Lodge, Toronto, near the premises (if by letter post-paid).

Toronto, July 6, 1860   3199-6t

Advertisement from the July 6, 1860, *Globe* newspaper in which John George Howard offers his country villa known as Sunnyside for sale.

as far west as the Humber River. Included in the commission's waterfront redevelopment plan (haven't I heard that expression just recently?) was the old Humber Bay. The commissioners had this part of the waterfront reclaimed using fill from the bottom of the old bay dressed with thousands of tons of clean topsoil from Pickering Township. A new thoroughfare, known as Boulevard Drive, was then constructed. It came complete with a mile-and-a-half-long, 24-foot-wide wooden boardwalk that allowed pedestrians to promenade along the water's edge all the way from Dowling Avenue to the Humber.

Then came the rides, dozens of them, little fast-food places, shooting galleries, a miniature golf course (called Lilliput golf back then), and a large change house known as the Sunnyside Bathing Pavilion, where visitors who wished to swim in the "new" Humber Bay could change into their bathing costumes. It was on the front steps of this magnificent new structure (thankfully, it still stands) that the official opening ceremonies of the new Sunnyside Amusement Park took place on June 28, 1922. The park's last full season was in 1955. The justifications for its demise included lack of interest and ever-increasing traffic on the boulevard (now called Lake Shore Boulevard West).

Several years ago I wrote a book entitled *I Remember Sunnyside*. It's been reprinted several times (most recently by Dundurn Press), but in each reprint I was never able to come up with the exact derivation of the term *Sunnyside*. Sure, I knew the immediate area around the park was called Sunnyside and that all 108 acres of this mostly forested

Rare photo of John George Howard's Sunnyside Villa, date unknown. It stood where the main entrance to St. Joseph's Health Centre is today and gave its name to this part of Toronto.

countryside were annexed by the city on January 2, 1888. However, it wasn't until I recently came across the accompanying advertisement in the *Globe* newspaper of July 6, 1860, that the actual origin of the word became evident.

As the ad explains, Sunnyside was the "beautiful suburban villa" of John George Howard, who owned nearby High Park and lived in Colborne Lodge. Howard built Sunnyside in the late 1840s on the sunny side of a hill (is this the precise origin of its name?), and his villa and the surrounding property quickly became the focal point for picnickers seeking refuge from the hot city streets a mile or so to the east. Over the years Sunnyside had many owners, including the Sisters of St. Joseph, who for a while used the old building as an orphanage. It was finally demolished in 1945, and part of what is now St. Joseph's Health Centre was erected on the site.

July 27, 2003

Ferry Across the Bay

The very first ferry boat began operating across Toronto Bay in 1833. Called the *Sir John of the Peninsula* (no doubt in honour of Sir John Colborne, the provincial lieutenant governor of the day), the contraption was rated at two horsepower simply because it was propelled by two horses. The steeds propelled the strange vessel by walking in place on a treadmill that in turn was connected by gears to side paddles and thereby giving the unusual craft its motive power. The route was from the foot of Church Street to a wharf in front of a rudimentary hotel run by Michael O'Connor. Now, with this convenient connection in place, the public was able to access the pleasures of Toronto Island.

Over the next 17 decades a number of other modes of getting to and from the Island have been promoted, including but not limited to a bridge from the foot of Bathurst Street, especially for streetcars; a vehicle followed by a pedestrian-only tunnel under the West Gap; and even an aerial ride (like the one that used to operate at the Canadian National Exhibition) over the Eastern Gap. And while that bridge idea has been resurrected in a different form, the city-owned and -operated ferry boats continue to be the only way for the public to get there and back.

Historically, Michael O'Connor, the owner of the first hotel on the Island, can be considered as one of Toronto Island's earliest benefactors,

Wiman Baths on Toronto Island, a gift to Torontonians from Erastus Wiman.

The *Erastus Wiman*, named for the former Torontonian, carried passengers between Manhattan and Staten Island. (Photo courtesy Staten Island ferry historian Trevor Gherardi; see *www.siferry.com*)

but there was another fellow who was an even greater supporter. Erastus (boy, they don't give out first names like that anymore) Wiman was born in 1834 in Churchville, a small town near Brampton, Upper Canada. He was educated in Toronto where he earned a few dollars as a newsboy. Eventually he became a printer's apprentice, then commercial editor for the *Globe* newspaper. In 1859 he tried his hand at municipal politics, serving a term as councilman for St. Andrew's Ward.

But it was his business acumen that resulted in an offer to join the prestigious American firm R.G. Dun and Company (now Dun & Bradstreet). In 1867 Wiman became the influential firm's general manager and moved to the United States, taking up residence in a large mansion on Staten Island. While with the Dun organization he worked hard to develop various interests of his own all over the island. These included a successful commuter steam railway line and major real-estate holdings. Of special note was his presidency of the highly lucrative Staten Island Ferry Company that continues to provide service between Manhattan and Staten Island. In fact, one of the company's ferry boats was named for this Toronto boy.

During his rise to prominence, Wiman never forgot the city that gave him his start. Recognizing the popularity of public baths in New York City in 1882, he funded what was to be known as the Wiman Baths, a public bathing facility located at the east end of Toronto Island. Although it doesn't sound like much in our modern world where bathtubs and showers are common fixtures in virtually every household, in a more innocent Toronto these public baths were a godsend for the ordinary man, woman, and child. For just a few pennies citizens were given the opportunity to cleanse themselves of the filth and grime accumulated during long days of hard work.

Erastus Wiman died in the community of St. George on Staten Island in 1904.

Readers wishing to learn more about the story of the Wiman Baths and Toronto Island history are invited to an open house at the Toronto Island Archives, 5 Ojibway Avenue, Algonquin Island, every Sunday afternoon from 1:00 to 5:00 p.m. For more details, email archivist Albert Fulton at *archives9@rogers.com*.

August 3, 2003

All Aboard ... Eventually

On August 11, 1927, Toronto salesman D.A. Moore of 17 Langley Avenue became the first person to buy a railway ticket at Toronto's sparkling new Union Station. To be historically correct, however, Moore's ticket wasn't actually the first to be issued. That one had gone to Prince Edward, the Prince of Wales who, with his younger brother, George, had officially opened the station a few days earlier. This incident, filled with pomp and circumstance as most of the events the extremely popular Prince of Wales took part in were, was choreographed to be part of the boys' trip to Edward's ranch in Alberta.

Officials thought that since the prince and his brother would be in Toronto, anyway, why not have them open the new station before starting their train trip out west. To be completely honest, the station wasn't really ready — far from it, in fact. But what the heck, the boys are in town. Let's do it!

So at 10:30 on the morning of August 6, 1927, Edward, who had arrived the previous evening, entered the station. He and his brother were each given two pairs of tickets, the first from a Canadian National Railways ticket agent, and the second, the ones they would ostensibly use to get to their destination, from a beaming Canadian Pacific Railway employee. Edward then proceeded to cut a red satin ribbon strung across the tracks before walking over to the main entrance where he unlocked one of the doors with a gold key.

In the hubbub the prince was heard to make some comment to his aides about how North Americans designed their railway terminals in the form of temples to the gods (weren't railway owners like gods, anyway?) before quickly making for an open car parked on Front Street in which he was paraded through the downtown streets before attending a civic reception.

With its train sheds unfinished and railway tracks nowhere in sight in this 1927 view, Toronto's new Union Station, though virtually complete, remained unusable by the general public. The clock tower of the old Union Station is in the foreground.

It looked like Toronto's new Union Station was finally open. Actually, it wasn't. Once the prince was out of the way the doors were locked once again and the "temple" stood empty for another five days until Mr. Moore stepped up and bought the first genuine ticket.

Interestingly, this stutter-step opening of Union Station was pretty much indicative of the way Torontonians got this magnificent station in the first place.

History tells us that Toronto has had a Union Station of sorts since 1855 when the Grand Trunk (the second railway to serve Toronto, the Ontario, Simcoe, and Huron, or Northern, being the first in 1853) and Great Western railways shared, for a time, a small building on the south side of Front Street at Bay. This structure was replaced by a two-storey wooden building in 1858. Even after the Great Western moved eight years later into its own station (where the Hummingbird Centre stands today), the old building continued to be referred to as Toronto's "Union Station."

Over the following years passenger traffic grew so rapidly that Grand Trunk officials had to build yet another station to handle the business. This Union Station ("Union," though still only one occupant) was south of Front Street and west of York and opened on July 1, 1873.

Throughout the next decade the number of railway companies increased. One of them, the new Canadian Pacific Railway, was allowed to use the facilities of the Grand Trunk, and in so doing finally gave legitimacy to the station being called a true "Union" station. The 1873 station was upgraded several times in an attempt to keep up with the burgeoning railway traffic, but space limitations restricted the size of the station and its ability to handle the crowds.

Finally, railway officials saw a glimmer of hope. On the evening of April 19, 1904, a fire erupted in a building near the Bay and Wellington corner. By the time the conflagration was out, a huge swath of land on the south side of Front Street between Bay and York was a smouldering wasteland. As far as the Grand Trunk and Canadian Pacific railways were concerned, this was the site of a new and much-needed Union Station for Toronto.

Remember, the year was 1904.

It took nearly a full decade of discussing, arguing, and even pleading before any sign of a new station materialized. That occurred on July 30, 1913, when the federal Board of Railway Commissioners issued a work order authorizing the start of construction on the $14-million station. Eight months later the plans as prepared by the architectural firm Ross and Macdonald, assisted by H.G. Jones of Montreal and Toronto's own John Lyle, were complete. The first shovel bit into the ground on September 26, 1914.

But in the meantime war had broken out in Europe and work on the station had a very low priority, so it took another half-dozen or so years to complete the building. Finally, the officials announced that the station was ready. Except, that is, for the fact that the tracks were nowhere in sight. Continued bickering between the railways and all levels of government had resulted in the elevated railway track viaduct being far from completion.

So even though the prince and Mr. Moore were able to get out by train in 1927, it would be nearly four more years before Toronto's Union Station was in full operation.

August 10, 2003

Meet You at the Station

A nd the "Saga of Union Station" continues ...

Earlier I traced the history of Toronto's temple-like railway station up to the time the Prince of Wales officially opened the place (on August 6, 1927) and the day D.A. Moore bought the first ticket. (The latter event took place five days later. Moore was obviously a souvenir hunter since his destination was the old Don station just a few miles away.)

While the railway companies were busily selling tickets, the station still wasn't fully functional, at least not in the way the planners had anticipated. That was all due to the ongoing fight between Canadian National Railways, Canadian Pacific Railway, the federal authorities, and the city over rail access to and from the new station. Because the station had been designed as a "through" station rather than a "terminal" where the tracks would terminate, it was necessary to raise the rail corridor along the waterfront onto a viaduct in order to eliminate the dangerous railway crossings affecting many of the city's major north-south streets in the downtown area. This grade separation would allow traffic and pedestrians to pass safely under the busy tracks. But until the grade separation was complete, passengers would continue to face long walks from the new station to the trains waiting on the old tracks many hundreds of yards to the south.

Unfortunately, as far as that grade separation was concerned, it was years in the future since neither railway was eager to spend the estimated $28.5 million necessary to complete such a massive project. (Interestingly, this figure was many times the price of the station itself.) In fact, the CPR was so upset with this multimillion-dollar proposal that it decided to abandon the waterfront altogether and build a station of its own at the north end of the city. To be known as the CPR North Toronto Station, this facility was only in operation as a train station for less than 15 years when the company had a change of heart and decided to join the CNR in the main downtown station. The North Toronto Station of 1916 now enjoys a new career as a gloriously restored liquor store.

An aerial view of Union Station, circa 1926, showing the Bay Street level crossing that existed before the elevated viaduct was built.

As for that controversial railway viaduct (the one we still walk and drive over — Bathurst to Spadina, and under, York to Eastern Avenue — today), a cost-sharing arrangement was eventually reached. The elusive viaduct was completed in late 1930, allowing the now not-so-new Union Station to fulfill its promise as one of the continent's finest railway stations.

Union Station now embarks on a new phase of its existence with Toronto City Council's recent decision (not without more controversy, something the station's familiar with) to enter into a 100-year lease with the Union Pearson Group that will result in the restoration and revitalization of the station proper along with the enhancement of its transportation functions. Stay tuned.

August 17, 2003

Electric Exhibits

This column wasn't something I had planned to write, obviously, just as no one had planned for Toronto's electrical power to fail so dramatically as it did the other day. However, as I sat in the dark I couldn't help but reflect on how ironic it was that one of the things the Canadian National Exhibition has promoted so vigorously over the years, "electricity, the wonder of the age," would return one day to haunt the "Grand Old Lady by the Lake." Haunting her to the extent of forcing the postponement of the fair's 125th anniversary party.

The photographs that accompany this column (all through the courtesy of the CNE Archives) depict just a few of the ways in which the CNE and electricity joined together to entertain and educate the public.

August 24, 2003

Prior to 1882, the use of electricity throughout the city of Toronto was limited and very much a novelty with gas still the main source of illumination. Early that year the directors of what was then known as the Toronto Industrial Exhibition (the name change would occur several decades later) decided to contract with two pioneer American companies to light the grounds and buildings with arc lights with additional lighting beacons atop towering masts scattered across the grounds. The electrical power was generated by dynamos connected by belts to what was described as a huge coal-fired automatic cut-off engine in the fair's Machinery Hall. That the experiment was a total success is confirmed by the fact that for the first time the grounds could stay open past 6:00 p.m. In a statement delivered on the final day of the 1882 fair, officials recorded that introduction of the electric light "served a most useful purpose in enabling many to see the exhibits who would otherwise have been unable to do so." The light beacon tower can be seen in the background of this circa 1882 photo from the CNE Archives.

Although television had been seen at the CNE in the early 1930s, it was still experimental. Nevertheless, crowds were amazed by the pictures they saw. Then, in 1939, sets that the public could actually purchase were put on display in the RCA Victor booth in the Electrical and Engineering Building (an impressive structure that stood where the National Trade Centre is today).

Each year the Dufferin Gate at the west end of the grounds welcomed crowds with intricate designs created using hundreds of electric light bulbs. The CNE's Diamond Jubilee exhibition was in 1938. This entrance was replaced by the present parabolic arch at the foot of Dufferin Street in 1959.

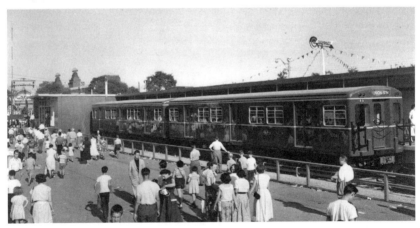

Electrically powered transportation vehicles were frequently shown to the general public first at the CNE. In fact, the continent's first electric streetcar was previewed in 1883 and perfected, with the now-common under-running trolley pole two years later. The Peter Witt, as well as the PCC and today's CLRV and ALRV streetcars, was also previewed at the Ex. In this view, taken at the 1953 edition of the CNE, Toronto's modern new English-built subway cars (that would enter service the following year with the opening on March 30 of the new Yonge subway) were a major attraction.

How Rexdale Was Born

The name Rexdale has been in the news recently, unfortunately for reasons I'd rather not dwell on except to quote the old adage that a few bad apples spoil the barrel. Of course, the vast majority of those who call Rexdale home are hard-working, law-abiding citizens simply trying to make ends meet. The genius behind the creation of Rexdale nearly a half-century ago was himself a hard-working, law-abiding citizen who got in on the suburban housing boom. It occurred on the outskirts of many large North American cities on the continent during the years that followed the end of the Second World War. Vacant land in the city core was at a premium, and it wasn't long before entrepreneurs saw the future in developing housing subdivisions on farmland on the city outskirts. Locally, businessman and entrepreneur E.P. Taylor got the ball rolling in 1954 with his innovative Don Mills development.

Then, a few years later, the 50-year-old son of an Etobicoke Township farmer got his chance. Rex Wesley Heslop was born in 1905 on a farm located on the east side of today's Islington Avenue, just north of today's Highway 401. Rex worked with his father in the family construction business before making his way to Detroit where he drove a cab for a time. He then decided to try his hand as a new car salesman, eventually becoming one of the best in the entire State of Michigan.

But Heslop still hadn't found his niche in life, so he moved on, this time all the way north to the mines in Northern Ontario, where

Above: aerial view looking northwest at the first phase of the new Rexdale subdivision in 1955. The Islington Avenue and Rexdale Boulevard intersection is at top left. Inset: land developer Rex Heslop, the father of Rexdale, directs efforts via one of two mobile telephones in his Cadillac in 1956.

he was hurt in a rock slide. He then returned to Toronto where he once again took up employment in the construction business. After a stint working for others, Heslop decided to go out on his own and, with a modest loan from a local banker, put a $112 down payment on four-and-a-half building lots in the Alderwood area of Etobicoke. He converted these lots to six smaller lots on which he built a half-dozen homes, each of which he listed at $7,000. They sold even before house number 6 was finished.

Before many days had passed, the confident builder had acquired the land in question for $110,000. Soon streets, water mains, and sewers were being laid out on land that until recently had been covered by semi-prosperous farms. Next came rows and rows of houses that listed for either $9,000 or $10,000 each. Sales were brisk and, in short order, 330 families were calling Rexdale home. To serve their every need, Heslop also built one of the area's first and, for a time, largest shopping centres. The Rexdale Shopping Centre opened in 1956, four years after the city's first, Sunnybrook (at Bayview and Eglinton avenues), and three years after Lawrence Plaza (at Bathurst Street and Lawrence Avenue). By the time Heslop's plaza opened, Rexdale itself had grown to include more than 3,600 homes and some 70 industries.

Heslop tried a similar venture farther west in Georgetown where he created another subdivision, this time naming it Delrex, combining his first name with that of his wife, Delma. This time, however, the developer ran into serious problems, mostly of a political nature. Tired of name-calling and in-fighting, Rex Heslop, now 61, sold his interest and retired. This pioneer land developer passed away on September 30, 1973.

August 31, 2003

Get Your Motor Running

The question as to whether the price of gas is too high or too low has perplexed the Canadian public for decades. In fact, not since those far-off days when gasoline was regarded as a worthless by-product of the refining of oil and thrown away has anyone really been happy with its price. Early in the 20th century there were frequent news stories comparing gasoline prices for the same brand of fuel here and in Buffalo, New York. Invariably, the cost per gallon was less across the border, even when the Canadian dollar was at par or at a premium against the American greenback. This discrepancy usually led to newspaper stories that claimed price gouging was going on. Just as often, however, were statements put out by the gas companies refuting the allegation. The excuse given for the different prices for a gallon of gas offered by the same manufacturers was that the fuels were, in fact, different. Ours was more expensive since it was refined to a higher quality because our weather characteristics were more demanding. Whatever those words meant, it sure sounded plausible. Oh, well ... fill 'er up, Mac!

With gas rationing during the Second World War the price per gallon was no longer a concern. It was fixed by the government. But with the return of better times something new happened — the gasoline price war. First one station would drop the price, then the nearby outlet would meet that new price or better it by a penny. The guy up the street, not to be left out, dropped it another two cents, and on it went. Then, as suddenly as it started, it ended with everyone at the same level. A week or two later and it would happen all over again. In the photo on the next page, taken in early 1956, a gasoline price war has broken out downtown. The station shown in the photo was at the corner of Church and Dundas streets, and staff can be seen *pumping* gas. Interestingly, this Esso outlet remains on the corner but is now self-serve, a type of station introduced in the early 1970s. In 1969 there were none; just six years later there were nearly 500 across Ontario.

Remember Joy gasoline? The company ads, such as this one from 1938, often took the form of cartoons.

At last look this particular station was selling gas at 79.5 cents a litre, an almost tenfold increase over the 1956 price. By the way, in the background of this same photo is the old Mutual Street Arena. This building was the Toronto Maple Leafs hockey team's first home rink. Years after the photo was taken the station was extensively remodelled and renamed the Terrace, then demolished.

One of the major differences between the gas stations of today and those of yesteryear really has to do with the number of companies in

Gas-price war at the Dundas and Church Esso station, 1956. Drivers wait patiently as the attendants fill 'em up at 36 cents a *gallon*!

the business. For instance, today we can count the number of major brands on one hand: Esso, Sunoco, Petro-Canada, and Shell — that's pretty much it. Not that many years ago that number was much higher. Who remembers, in addition to those already mentioned, stations selling Texaco, BP, FINA, Supertest, City Service, BA or, if you're a little older, Silver Flash, Regent, Good Rich, Perfection, Reliance, White Rose and, of course, Joy gasoline?

The last company was the brainchild of Charles Austin of Detroit, Michigan. His wife, Margaret, brought the company to Canada in the mid-1930s and began selling, at reduced prices, cheap Romanian gasoline that had been tankered to Montreal for refining. Perhaps the best-remembered feature of the little Joy stations, of which there were 12 in Toronto, 11 in Detroit, and five in Montreal, was the look of the buildings. Each station resembled a small castle. In later years the Hercules people (the same crowd that ran the war surplus store on Yonge Street) acquired the stations. Before long both the company and the stations were history, except for one former Joy station at the corner of Windermere and Lake Shore Boulevard.

Even its future is questionable.

September 7, 2003

"New" City Hall Aging

Although it's now several decades old, we still refer to Toronto's City Hall as "new," in deference to "Old" City Hall just across the street. Actually, if a few city politicians and land developers had had their way back when the first Eaton Centre plans were presented (originally known as the Viking Project), there would be no reason to call the present one "new," since there would have been no "old." It was only through the perseverance of a few public-spirited citizens that the ancient building continues to grace Toronto's downtown core.

For those of us who were present at the official dedication ceremony on September 13, 1965, it just doesn't seem possible that four decades have slipped by since Governor General Georges Vanier did the honours when he used scissors to cut a 100-foot-long, four-foot-wide red ribbon to officially open Finnish architect Viljo Revell's magnificent creation. Seconds later five Royal Canadian Air Force CF-101 Voodoo jet fighters screamed overhead, offering their noisy salute to Toronto's "New" City Hall.

Present at the ceremony were five previous Toronto mayors (Billy Stewart, Leslie Saunders, Ralph Day, Bert Wemp, and Nathan Phillips). Phillips, after whom the civic square in front of the building is named, served as mayor from 1955 to 1962 and was the prime mover in getting a new municipal building for Toronto after decades of wrangling.

Toronto's "New" City Hall appears through the rubble as the old Casino Theatre on the south side of Queen Street is flattened by the wreckers. The Sheraton Centre now stands on the site. The photo was taken in July 1965, just two months before the new hall was officially opened.

Also present were Prime Minister Lester Pearson ("Toronto now has a City Hall as modern as Toronto, indeed as modern as the day after tomorrow"), Mayor Phil Givens ("The building is symbolic of the vitality of the city, symbolic of bold audacity, for it took audacity to build such an untraditional building in a city so steeped in tradition"), and Abe Gowler, a 91-year-old former Torontonian who came all the way from Victoria, British Columbia, to be part of the festivities. His quote for members of the press was: "I can remember when I used to play baseball where the 'Old' City Hall stands."

The official opening program was followed by a week of festivities, with the Toronto Symphony and Canadian Opera Company present on Tuesday night, square dancing on the Square on Wednesday, school choirs on Thursday, and a short version of *Nationbuilders* that had been performed at the Canadian National Exhibition earlier in the month. To top it all off, Saturday night featured *Toronto A-GO-GO*, starring Bobby Curtola, David Clayton Thomas, and Little Caesar and the Consuls, Canadian music icons of the day.

Even "Old" City Hall across the street has something new to boast about. The quartet of gargoyles high atop its clock tower are back.

Not to be outdone, "Old" City Hall across the street, now more than a century old, has its quartet of gargoyles back. Part of the original building when it opened on September 18, 1899, the gargoyles were removed for safety reasons in the 1930s. Today, thanks to the expertise of the Ventin Group, restoration architects on the "Old" City Hall project, the gargoyles, now cast from bronze (the originals were sandstone), are back, high atop the clock tower.

September 14, 2003

A Make-Work Project

The use of the word *depression*, as in the Great Depression of 1929, usually conjures up stories of a truly depressing nature: men out of work, families being thrown out of their houses, bread and soup lines, No Help Wanted signs, and the like. But as bad as the world-wide depression of the late 1920s through the 1930s was, a few good things came out of it. Things like public-works projects that probably would never have been given the go-ahead without the need to get able-bodied men back to work.

One of the best examples in Toronto (and there are many) is the short stretch of University Avenue between Queen and Front streets. While there's no doubt that increasing vehicular traffic would have eventually forced the city to extend University Avenue south a couple of blocks to connect with Front Street (it originally dead-ended at Queen), it was the arrival of the Great Depression that got that extension built sooner rather than later.

Although the idea of extending the street to Front was agreed to by all members of City Council, the actual route that the extension would take became the subject of controversy. Some politicians and one of the city's afternoon newspapers wanted it laid out so as to enter Front Street opposite Union Station. This plan would have seen several buildings flanking the new street dramatically increase in value.

The right-of-way for the extension of University Avenue south of Queen Street is plainly visible in this view looking north from Front Street. Note the absence of heavy machinery in favour of using unemployed men. Note also the new Canada Life Building in the centre background. It was anticipated that all new buildings erected on what many believed would be Toronto's Champs-Élysées would be of a similar or higher architectural treatment.

Mayor William Stewart does the honours on November 1, 1931, as he officially opens the new Queen-to-Front stretch of University Avenue. Leopold Macauley, the provincial minister of highways, is at the other end of the ribbon. Note also the newspaper boy and perhaps an out-of-work war amputee also getting in on the act.

Others, including the editorial staff of the powerful *Evening Telegram* newspaper, insisted that a more direct route to Front be taken. The latter bunch eventually won the day with the new street intersecting Front well west of the York Street corner. Many more years would pass before another re-alignment would result in the Front-York-University configuration that confuses out-of-towners (and many locals) to this very day.

For the record, the enabling bylaw for the extension was approved on September 1930, with the actual start of work on the $5.8-million project (today that figure might get you 20 yards of highway plus three catch basins) commencing on March 21, 1931. On that day wrecking crews made up of dozens of unemployed men (heavy wrecking machinery was frowned upon in favour of real manpower) began demolishing the old buildings that stood on the right-of-way to be followed by the new street.

Less than 20 months later, November 1, 1931, to be precise, Mayor William Stewart (who succeeded Mayor Bert Wemp, who got the ball rolling during his term of office) cut the ribbon to officially open the University Avenue Extension.

September 21, 2003

Moving with the Times

Toronto's Upper Canada College is one of the oldest educational institutions in Canada. It is also the oldest independent school in the Province of Ontario, having been established in 1829 by Sir John Colborne, the lieutenant governor of what was then called the Province of Upper Canada (a name that would be changed to Ontario in 1867, coincident with the creation of the new Dominion of Canada).

It was Colborne, one of the Duke of Wellington's generals at the Battle of Waterloo, who gave the new educational facility its original, and rather grandiose, title of Upper Canada College and Royal Grammar School. He intended that his school would fulfill a specific role, that of preparing the youth of the day, who had graduated from the province's various elementary-type schools, for a higher education that would be provided by a new provincial university (which has evolved into today's University of Toronto) that itself was coming closer to realization.

The site that the government set aside for Colborne's project was a small fraction of the nearly quarter-million acres of land it had earlier earmarked for educational purposes. In the case of the new Upper Canada College and Royal Grammar School that land was on the western edge of the Town of York, a community of about 7,000 souls that was still five years away from being elevated to city status (and renamed in the process).

Upper Canada College, 1831

The original Upper Canada College buildings at the northwest corner of King and Simcoe streets, circa 1831.

The school buildings were erected within the block bounded by today's King, John, Adelaide, and Simcoe streets. It was their presence at the northwest quadrant of the King and Simcoe intersection that eventually resulted in that particular corner taking on the term *Education*, while the other three corners took on the titles *Legislation*, *Salvation*, and *Damnation* because on them sat Government House, a church, and a tavern. Note that out of this quartet of buildings only *Salvation* remains in the form of the beautiful St. Andrew's Presbyterian Church.

Classes continued to be held on the *Education* corner for many years until members of the provincial legislature decreed that the college was no longer entitled to the property it occupied. In an article written on the occasion of Upper Canada College's 94th birthday, some anonymous scribbler suggested the old college had fallen out of favour because it was "sapping income from the University of Toronto."

Nothing daunted, UCC supporters made sure the school would continue uninterrupted by acquiring a parcel of land in an area of suburban Toronto known as Deer Park, so-called because of the many deer that roamed the area. It was here that UCC relocated in 1891.

Although of no relevance at the time, or for many years afterwards for that matter, the Deer Park location eventually became a major impediment as the number of vehicles using Avenue Road as a route to get into and out of the city rapidly increased. As the problem got worse, plans were made to move the school lock, stock, barrel, and chalkboards.

UPPER CANADA COLLEGE—TORONTO, CAN

Picture postcard of Upper Canada College a few years after its move to the Deer Park (Avenue Road) site in 1891.

The first of these plans surfaced nearly a century ago when it was announced by school officials that more than 500 acres of land on the Credit River, between Brampton and Georgetown and not far from the pretty little community of Norval, had been purchased for $66,000. At the same time it was revealed that the school was to receive more than $1 million for the 50-plus-acre Avenue Road site. A major player in the project, the Suydam Realty Company of Toronto, even drew up plans to subdivide a section of the school site into housing lots. Those same plans called for an extension of Avenue Road northwards through the property. The whole thing fell through, however, and the school continued at its Deer Park location. Incidentally, the school kept the Norval property, which it now operates as an outdoor education and environmental studies facility.

Then, in 1929, another plan surfaced that would have seen a good portion of the school moved to what was called the Van Nostrand Property to the north and east of the Yonge Street and York Mills Sideroad intersection. But, once again, relocation plans suffered a setback with the onset of the Great Depression. Financial constraints quickly put an end to the York Mills project. In fact, in the spring of 1932, all plans to move from the Deer Park site vanished when major improvements to the existing facilities were undertaken thanks to a $400,000 grant presented to UCC by the Massey Foundation.

September 28, 2003

Never on a Sunday

One day, not so long ago, I arrived at the *Toronto Sun* to be told there was a large package waiting for me in the mailroom. Actually, the term *large* is misleading. It was, in fact, a *LARGE* package postmarked Calgary, Alberta, with no other identification. It hadn't come collect, so I proceeded to open it. I soon found out that the item had been sent to me from John Dolan, a long-time friend and radio personality at CFRB (and several other Toronto stations), who left Toronto for the West some years earlier. I had recently done some local historical snooping for a project John was working on, and in appreciation of my hard work (either that or he was trying to clear his basement) he sent me the newspaper box to add to my collection "Toronto-iana." In a note John advised me that the box was actually the one located in front of the building in which CFRB had (and still has) its studios. Apparently, once all of the final-day *Telegrams* were sold, the vendor gave his favourite customer, the one who always smiled and offered the best tips, the box as a souvenir. How John got it, I don't know.

As I ripped away at the packing tape and tore open the cardboard (it was just like Christmas), what to my wondrous eyes did appear, but one of the old *Telegram* newspaper boxes that were familiar sights on Toronto street corners until the paper folded (literally) on October 30, 1971. But this was more than just any old *Telegram* news box. What caught my eye were the words *Daily — Sunday*.

Back in the 1940s and 1950s Toronto, indeed the whole province, was kept on the straight and narrow by some pretty far-reaching bylaws that affected just about anything one might want to do on Sunday. For instance, shopping in the vast majority of stores was out, and playing or even watching sports were no-noes, as was going to the movies. And few, if any, of the regular restaurants bothered opening on Sunday (I'm told hotel dining rooms did a brisk business on Sunday). Of course, one could read a newspaper on Sunday, but it couldn't be one published on that day.

Sunday newspapers were deemed by some, and in particular the Lord's Day Alliance, as being in contravention of the Lord's Day Act as

Policeman tickets a *Telegram* newsboy for selling papers on a Sunday, in this case a first day *Sunday Telegram*. Later it was admitted this was actually a "staged" photograph.

passed by the federal government in 1906. The act prohibited people from working on Sunday. Putting a Sunday paper together and selling it involved work. Therefore, ipso facto, in the minds of the Alliance members at least, the upstart *Sunday Telegram* was unlawful. The Alliance requested that the province's attorney general, Kelso Roberts, and his officials investigate the matter. It was then that the Ontario Provincial Police, as well as members of the Metropolitan Toronto Police, swung into action. Not only did they investigate the *Telegram*, but several other Toronto newspapers, one private radio station, and the federal government's own Canadian Broadcasting Corporation.

However, in the case of the *Telegram* at least, the whole exercise was for naught. The investigation went slowly (it seems the Lord's Day Alliance people were the only ones fired up) and before any charge was laid against the newspaper, John Bassett, the chairman and publisher of the *Telegram*'s daily and Saturday editions and the brain behind the Sunday version, ordered the publishing of the *Sunday Telegram* terminated. He cited low circulation and the scarcity of advertisers willing to take a chance with ads on Sunday in staid, old Toronto. The experiment lasted from March 17 to July 28, 1957, a mere 20 weeks. Another 16 years would pass before the *Sunday Sun* began to shine over Toronto.

* * *

One of Canada's most interesting museums finally has a permanent home. Although housed for the past few years in De Havilland Aircraft of Canada's 1929 factory located in Downsview Park, the Toronto Aerospace Museum's continuing presence in this historic structure has been uncertain. Until recently, that is. Successful negotiating on the part of the landlord and officials of the museum has resulted in Downsview Park becoming the permanent home of this interesting, entertaining, and educational showplace that features many of the triumphs realized during Canada's long and honourable aviation history. Some of the attractions on view include a soon-to-be-completed full-size model of the Avro Arrow, ongoing restoration of the famous Lancaster bomber FM-104 (formerly on display opposite the Canadian National Exhibition Grounds), and a number of aircraft previously in service with the Royal Canadian Air Force and the Royal Canadian Navy. Visit *www.torontoaerospacemuseum.com* for more information.

October 5, 2003

Tunnel Vision

One of the nicest men I ever met, and one of the most politically astute, was the late Allan Lamport. "Lampy" served Toronto in a variety of elected positions — alderman, controller, and mayor in both the "Old" and "New" City Halls — in a career that lasted from 1937 to 1972. Whenever I was in his presence I would try to get Allan to reminisce about how the city had changed during his time in office. He often took the bait and gave me insights into a Toronto I never knew. He, of course, championed Sunday sports (a revolutionary idea that led to the present-day concept of open Sundays), and that was something he certainly loved to talk about.

During a chat we had shortly before his death in late 1999 at the age of 97, he made a comment about modern-day municipal politics. It was a statement I'll never forget, and one that rings even truer today as Torontonians look for someone to take over the helm of a city that has become akin to a rudderless ship. "Lampy" said that today's Toronto is a great city not because of what has been done in recent years, but rather as a result of what had been set in motion many years ago by elected officials who had the city's future, not their own, in their minds and hearts. That dedication seems to be missing these days.

While several of those insightful politicians from years gone by come to mind ("Lampy" being one), one of the most perceptive city politicians of yesteryear had to have been Horatio Clarence Hocken, who was born in Toronto in 1857. His schooling was of the abbreviated variety, with young Horatio entering the working world right out of public school. Hocken's first real job was in the newspaper business where he quickly became a top-notch typesetter, a position that necessitated great manual dexterity as well as quick fingers, mind, and feet. Perhaps that's how he obtained his unusual nickname. While his proper first name was Horatio, to most of his co-workers he was "Race" Hocken.

Horatio went on to hold several positions at the old *Toronto News*. But when the newspaper introduced the automatic typesetting machine, Hocken led the printers out on strike, an action that resulted in the creation in 1892 of an opposition paper, one that we know today as the *Toronto Star*. Hocken became that upstart journal's first business manager.

In 1907 "Race" Hocken announced he was going to try his hand at municipal politics, but rather than getting his feet wet as an alderman (which was the usual way) he would try for the much-loftier position of city councillor. As Horatio C. Hocken (a name he believed looked better on the election ballot), he won first time out and was re-elected twice more in 1908 and 1909, municipal elections being annual events back then.

Horatio C. Hocken (1857–1937), pioneer proponent of subways in Toronto.

In 1910 he set his eyes on the mayor's chair, only to be defeated by Reginald Geary. As part of his unsuccessful mayoralty platform, Hocken put forward a plan to help alleviate downtown traffic congestion (yes, even then). His carefully thought-out idea called for the construction of an underground railway (called "tubes" back then, subways today) from the corner of Front and Bay streets (the site of the proposed new Union Station) to Yonge and St. Clair. The trains would operate through tunnels under Terauley Street (now that part of Bay Street north of Queen) and North Street (Bay north of College), jog northeast under Ramsden Park to Yonge, then head northwards again, terminating at St. Clair. The cost? Precisely $5,386,870.

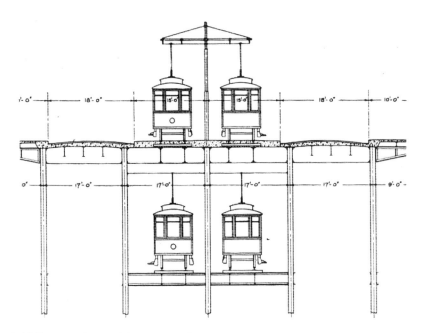

A 1912 report featured this concept for a street railway over the new Prince Edward Viaduct and a "tube" under it.

In March 1917, construction crews pose for the camera as the Prince Edward Viaduct nears completion. Note the provisions for a future subway under the roadbed.

Both Hocken and his far-sighted plan were defeated that year. Many reasons were given, the chief one being the fact that the surface lines were still under private ownership.

Geary went on to serve only one full term as mayor, resigning suddenly near the end of his second term to become corporation counsel for the city. Hocken, who had spent a year on the sidelines after his defeat and who had been returned as a controller in 1912, was selected by his fellow Board of Control members to step in as interim mayor following Geary's resignation. Horatio went on to serve as mayor in his own right for another two terms in 1913 and 1914.

Throughout his tenure as mayor, Hocken continued to promote his tube schemes, and while nothing ever happened, we can see a vestige of what was to come many years later (63, in fact, with the opening of the Bloor-Danforth subway in 1966) in the design of the Prince Edward (Bloor Street) Viaduct over the Don Valley.

American consulting engineer Bion J. Arnold agreed with the mayor's view that Toronto should be prepared to build tubes. In his 1912 report to City Council on Toronto traffic and transportation matters, Arnold even suggested that provision for a future tube be incorporated into the new viaduct on which construction would soon begin. Two of those provisions were a right-of-way under the roadbed and sufficient strength in the structure itself to support crowded subway trains.

Hocken went on to serve as MPP for Toronto Centre West from 1917 until his retirement in 1930. Four years later he was appointed to the Canadian Senate. "Race" Hocken died on February 19, 1937, a mere 36 hours after the passing of his wife of more than a half-century.

October 12, 2003

Swimming Towards Fame

I know you're not supposed to reveal a lady's age, so I won't. However, I will let you know that today is Marilyn Bell Di Lascio's birthday. You remember Marilyn, don't you? She was that unknown 16-year-old Toronto schoolgirl who upstaged the American swimming star Florence Chadwick back in the fall of 1954. Oops, I just gave away Marilyn's age, didn't I? Sorry, Marilyn.

The youngster's victory over Lake Ontario was one of the great Canadian stories of the 20th century. For those who weren't alive in early September 1954, the story went like this. Florence Chadwick had been contracted by the officials at the Canadian National Exhibition to swim the 32-mile stretch of cold, unforgiving Lake Ontario from the New York State shoreline, just east of the mouth of the Niagara River, to the CNE waterfront. It was to be one of the features of that year's exhibition. If the American long-distance swimming icon made it (as she surely would), she would be paid the lavish sum of $10,000 (in 1954 a top-of-the-line Ford or Chevy could be purchased for about $3,000). That prize money would easily be recouped from the thousands of people who would stream into the fairgrounds paying the 50-cent admission fee and hoping to see Florence make swimming history. And if she didn't complete the crossing, she wouldn't get a nickel. The CNE couldn't lose.

And, by the way, no one else need apply. As far as the CNE was concerned, it would be the American or no one.

The Marilyn Bell doll hit Eaton's Toyland shelves in time for Christmas 1954. And if you bought it on November 6, Marilyn was there to autograph her picture, no extra charge. Does anyone still have her Marilyn doll?

Young Marilyn, who was no slouch of a swimmer herself having won a number of national and international competitions, regarded the CNE's stance as anti-Canadian in the extreme. And she would do something about it. After discussing the matter with Gus Ryder, her coach at the Lakeshore Swimming Club, and her best friend, marathon swimmer Cliff Lumsden, Marilyn decided she, too, would attempt the lake crossing. But she wouldn't do it to compete with Florence, nor would she do it for the prize money. In fact, there wasn't anything at all in it for the Toronto-born 16-year-old. She'd simply do it for her country and for her friends at the swimming club.

As fate would have it, Florence wouldn't be in Marilyn's sights for very long. Less than seven hours after entering the cold lake, the American star became violently sick and was taken from the water. And while Florence would no longer challenge Marilyn, the cold, choppy lake and eels would.

Hours would pass as the youngster struggled with the lake, some-times gaining on it and other times seemingly defeated by it. But final-ly, almost 21 hours after she began her quest to prove Canadians were as good, and in some cases, better than Americans, Marilyn touched the seawall south of the Boulevard Club where thousands had gathered to meet and acclaim her the "Lady of the Lake." In fact, virtually the entire nation was in an uproar. Toronto's Marilyn Bell quickly became a Canadian icon. Hundreds showered her with gifts, and after a while even the CNE came across with the $10,000 prize money.

The following year, 1955, Marilyn conquered the English Channel, and in 1956 she swam the treacherous Strait of Juan de Fuca, which separates British Columbia from the State of Washington. While her hometown did honour her with the City of Toronto Civic Award of Merit (in fact, she received the very first such award), neither the province nor the country got around to recognizing her achieve-ments. But that will finally change later this week when the lieutenant governor, on behalf of the citizens of Ontario, presents Marilyn with the prestigious Order of Ontario.

As for the federal government, Canadians who remember those exciting days nearly a half-century ago are still waiting for some recog-nition from Ottawa. Something like the Order of Canada in time for the 50th anniversary of Marilyn's historic swim would be fitting.

* * *

It's less than a month until municipal Election Day, Monday, November 10, 2003. In an attempt to interest readers enough to get out and vote in what many believe is the most important of the trio of elections we have in this country, I've been offering for your perusal a look back at a few of Toronto's mayors of yesteryear.

This time around it's Thomas Foster, who served on City Council for 25 years, including 1925, 1926, and 1927 as mayor. Born on Vaughan Road in York Township in 1852, Foster grew up in the Uxbridge part of Southern Ontario. He entered the business world at a young age, investing what little money he had in a small Queen Street East butcher shop. The business grew and so, too, did Foster's reputa-tion for giving full value for money received. Everyone respected him, and before long he had earned the title of "Honest Tom." First elected to public office in 1891, it was reported that over his quarter-century in municipal politics his business acumen saved the city several million dollars. He also made sure no one at City Hall took advantage of the

This beautiful memorial just outside Uxbridge, Ontario, is the final resting place of Thomas Foster, who served on City Council for a quarter-century, including three one-year terms as the mayor of Toronto.

city's fleet of cars for personal use. He had the words *City of Toronto* emblazoned on each vehicle.

Foster never forgot his upbringing, and in 1935–36 erected the Foster Memorial Temple to honour not only his wife and daughter (who died at the age of 10) but all the pioneers of the district where he spent his childhood. The Foster Memorial, looking for all the world like a miniature Taj Mahal, is located on Durham Road 1 (Concession 7) just west of the Town of Uxbridge.

October 19, 2003

* Many who remember Marilyn Bell's numerous achievements are still puzzled that she has yet to be awarded the Order of Canada.

Under the Waterfront

When I worked at the Canadian National Exhibition in the 1970s, I became responsible for developing plans for the Ex's centennial-year fair that was to be held in 1978. One of the ideas I had was to run a ferry service from the docks at the foot of Bay Street to the CNE/Ontario Place waterfront. Actually, this really wasn't a new idea. A century earlier all kinds of passenger vessels ran to and from the Toronto Industrial Exhibition (the CNE's original name), docking at the old wooden wharf at the foot of Dufferin Street.

During my discussions with staff of the Toronto Harbour Commission about the idea, I frequently chatted with Jack Jones, the commission's chief engineer. Jack had several ideas on how to implement a safe routing for the ferries from the protected harbour to a new dock to be built not far from where HMCS *Haida* was berthed. However, for a variety of reasons the project never got past the talking stage.

In the course of our discussions we occasionally got off the ferry-boat topic and began chatting about whether he thought some kind of connecting link between the city and the Island would ever be built.

As I've written in previous columns, the construction of what is now referred to as a "fixed link" is certainly not a new idea. In fact, the first recorded plan to build a mainland/Toronto Island connection that I've found took the form of a streetcar-only bridge. It was proposed in 1886 and would allow the city's less-affluent citizens access to the

Aerial view of Toronto Island showing locations of the present and a relocated Western Channel.

The "fixed link" connecting the city with the airport on Toronto Island is certainly not a new idea. This one, for pedestrians only, was proposed in the early 1960s.

Island for a single fare, not the two fares (one for the streetcar and one for the ferry boat) then necessary. When the proposal was read a little more closely, it became obvious that the real reason for the bridge was the hope that City Council would then permit the privately owned streetcar company to operate its vehicles on Sundays. Council saw through the scheme and turned it down flat. Sunday streetcars continued to be forbidden until approval was finally given in 1897.

In the years that have passed since that initial proposal, all manner of "fixed links" have been promoted, including tunnels under the Western Channel (the vehicle and pedestrian type as well as the pedestrian-only kind such as the one depicted in the sketch accompanying this column) and a variety of bridges. In addition, someone even proposed a chair-lift system similar to the old-fashioned Alpine Way that Conklin operated at the CNE for many years.

As Jack and I continued our chat, he told me what he would do to eliminate the fixed-link question once and for all. I've never forgotten his suggestion and have often wondered whether it would work. Now, with the bridge idea such a prominent topic in the current mayoralty race, I offer Jack's unique idea forthwith. By the way, the following assumes that the Toronto City Centre Airport remains in business. Whether it does or not is for people smarter than I am to decide.

Here is Jack's idea. Just as the present Western Channel is man-made (having been constructed in 1911 to provide a safer passage into and out of Toronto Harbour than that offered by the original Western Channel several hundred feet farther inland at the current Lake Shore Boulevard/Bathurst Street intersection), a new passage would be created by excavating a channel a short distance south of the airport. The fill from this excavation would be used to backfill the present Western Channel. That done the airport would be part of the mainland and would be easily accessible by road, rail, and foot. The safety issue would be settled while the newly dug Western Channel would ensure that both the airport and vehicle traffic from the city would continue to be isolated from Toronto Island.

Jack's idea is relatively simple, and perhaps that's why it has never been acted upon. Or has it? Be glad to receive any comments.

* * *

With the municipal election just a couple of weeks away, here's another brief profile of a Toronto mayor of yesteryear. The son of a Toronto market gardener, Fred Conboy attended city public and high schools, graduating with a degree in dentistry in 1904. His dental office was at Bloor and Westmoreland where he practised for more than 20 years before being appointed provincial director of dental services. He then turned to municipal politics where he served as a

Fred Conboy served as Toronto's mayor from 1941 to 1945. He also discovered the British schooner HMS *Nancy*, now a major attraction at Wasaga Beach.

member of the Board of Education. Later he was elected to City Council, serving two terms as alderman and four as controller. Dr. Conboy then entered the 1941 mayoralty race and was successful. He continued to serve as mayor for an additional three one-year terms, retiring after being defeated in the 1945 elections by Robert H. Saunders.

As a young man, Dr. Conboy spent many of his summers at Wasaga Beach. In the summer of 1924, he came across a cannonball buried in the bank of the Nottawasaga River. He spent the next two summers prowling the area and eventually unearthed (literally) the ruins of a sunken British armed schooner. It turned out that the charred hulk was that of HMS *Nancy*, which had been sunk by a trio of American ships during the War of 1812.

Conboy, assisted by C.H.J. Snider of the old *Evening Telegram* newspaper, was eventually able to convince the provincial government to take steps to preserve the remnants of this historic relic. Today the HMS *Nancy* Museum is one of the province's most popular War of 1812 attractions.

October 26, 2003

The Patron St. Lawrence

On November 5, 1803, a public market, the one we now know as the St. Lawrence Market, was held for the very first time. Initially, the market was nameless. The title St. Lawrence was tacked on once the Town of York was elevated to city status in 1834. For administrative purposes the new City of Toronto was divided into five wards named after St. George, St. Andrew, St. Patrick, St. David, and St. Lawrence. The first four honoured the patron saints of England, Scotland, Ireland, and Wales, while the last recognized the patron saint of Canada. Since the ward in which the market was located was St. Lawrence, the market's expanded name came about quite naturally. Interestingly, a second market, called St. Andrew's, was established years later on Queen Street West in St. Andrew's Ward. However, for a variety of reasons that market only lasted a short time and is now just a footnote in city history books.

The man we have to thank for the creation of the St. Lawrence Market is Peter Hunter, who served as Upper Canada's second lieutenant governor from 1799 until 1805. The first lieutenant governor, and the founder of what became Toronto, was John Graves Simcoe, who held the post from 1792 to 1794 before returning to England. Simcoe was followed by Peter Russell, who served as administrator until the appointment of Hunter. And while Simcoe and Russell have several local streets named in their honour, Hunter has none.

The St. Lawrence Hall, and in the distance the third market on this site. The first market opened on November 5, 1803.

As for the reason Hunter established a market in the first place, we only have to look at the preamble to the decree he signed on October 26, 1803, a mere 10 days before the first market officially opened: "Whereas great prejudice has arisen to the inhabitants of the town and township of York from no place or day having been set apart or appointed for the exposing for sale cattle, sheep, poultry and other provisions, goods and merchandise brought by merchants, farmers and others for the necessary supply of the said town of York; and whereas great benefit and advantage might be derived to the said inhabitants and others by establishing a weekly market within that town at a place and on a day certain for the purpose aforesaid; know all men that I do ordain, erect, establish and appoint a public open market to be held on Saturday in each and every week during the year on a certain plot or piece of land within that town ..." The Saturday selected was November 5, 1803.

Hunter went on to describe the market site in minute detail, in fact, far too detailed to record here. Suffice to say, the boundaries of the original five-and-a-quarter-acre market were the modern King, Church, Front, and Jarvis streets. Somehow over the ensuing 200 years that square has been nibbled away at, with shops, restaurants, offices, and condominiums now occupying the west end of the site. At the east end various buildings have been constructed, including the beautiful St. Lawrence Hall, which was opened in 1850 on the site of the old Town Hall. After York's elevation to a higher status, St. Lawrence Hall became the city's first City Hall by default. Since then Toronto has had three more. The wooden market buildings (originally described as "shambles") were eventually replaced by more substantial brick buildings, and in the late-1960s by the structure that we know today as the North Market.

To learn more about the St. Lawrence Market and its interesting history, visit the Market Gallery on the second floor of the South Market building.

November 2, 2003

Mayoral Elections

There is no doubt that tomorrow's municipal election in Toronto will be one of the most important in the city's history. In fact, so complex are the matters facing the next City Council and so diverse are the remedies being put forward by the dozens and dozens of contenders for the various municipal offices that if nothing else the next three years are going to be interesting. One thing we do know: if a community's strength comes from its sense of heritage and traditions, Toronto is in good shape to face the future.

I imagine the 9,000 Torontonians of the early 1830s were also concerned with the outcome of their municipal election. One reason for that concern was because the April 27, 1834, event was the new city's first. Until that year the future of the Town of York had been in the hands of appointed magistrates, and there had been very little chance that these officials would allow things to stray too far from the status quo, a situation that favoured members of the very unpopular Family Compact, a small group consisting of the well-heeled in town who had things pretty much their own way. A government responsible to the needs and desires of the general population was certainly not something members of the Family Compact were eager to see established.

The idea of giving the little town more control over its destiny by having annual general elections wasn't a new concept. In fact, some liberal-minded citizens (referred to as Reformers by many) suggested as early as 1822 that the town be made a city with the inherent right to hold general elections. So touchy was the subject to those in charge (the Family Compact, also known as Tories) that the matter was left unresolved until the passage on March 6, 1834, of "4th William IV, Chap. 23," described as an act to extend the limits of the Town of York, to erect the said town into a city, and to incorporate under the name of the City of Toronto. The prime intent of the act was to promote a "more efficient system of police and municipal government." And to accomplish that feat the act went on to state that provisions would be put in place for the citizenry to elect a mayor, aldermen, and common councilmen. The first municipal election in the new City of Toronto would be held on March 27, 1834, a mere three weeks after "4th William IV" was passed.

Toronto's first mayor, William Lyon Mackenzie. (Courtesy City of Toronto Archives)

The election would be "open," that is, anyone entitled to vote (and there were many restrictions, including property holdings, age,

For its City Hall the newly established Toronto inherited what had been used for years as little York's Town Hall. Portions of the building were also used as a market. The St. Lawrence Hall now sits on this site.

and sex, with only the male variety being eligible) would voice his selection verbally. Voting took place in the Court House on the north side of King Street just west of Church Street as well as in some of the young city's most popular hotels — Elliott's, Wright's, Falvey's, and Ontario House.

Dr. John Rolph, the man many people thought would be the newly created City of Toronto's first mayor. (Portrait from: *Rebel with Causes* by Dr. Charles Godfrey, Codam Publishing)

A total of 41 gentlemen ran as either Reformers or Tories for the positions of alderman and common councilman, with two of each to be elected for each of the five wards. (An alderman and common councilman appear to have had basically the same responsibilities.) Twenty elected officials would represent the city's 9,254 souls (one for every 462.7 citizens) for the next year and then they would do it all over again. As for the chief magistrate, or mayor, once the dust had settled he would be selected from the 20 elected members and would head the new council.

As concerned as the Family Compact people were with this major departure in the way things would be run, they were convinced they would hold on to power. Oops. When the election results were all in, the Reformers had elected 12 council members and the Tories eight. At first it seemed as if Reformer Dr. John Rolph, who was acceptable to most of the Tories, appeared to be headed for the mayor's chair. But when Rolph was informed that he didn't have total support, he left in a snit and never did serve. Worse still for the Tories, William Lyon Mackenzie, the most reviled of all the Reformers, was selected to lead the new council as the city's first mayor.

Toronto's first election was quite a heated event, though only a little blood was spilled. And what was the first thing on the new council's agenda? Where to get some money to fix the roads, actually the sidewalks. They got some, but not enough, so the wooden planks had to be laid lengthwise rather than crosswise to make the loan go further.

November 9, 2003

A Heavenly Venue

As some of my readers may be aware, I'm often asked to host bus tours of Toronto. Frequently, I suggest that as part of the tour we pay a visit to the beautiful St. Anne's Anglican Church on Gladstone Avenue just north of Dundas Street. That's because within the walls of this unique structure visitors will find some remarkable, and little known, work created by a few members of Canada's illustrious Group of Seven.

While the present church was constructed in 1907, the parish of St. Ann's (no final *e* at the time) had actually been established 45 years earlier to serve adherents of the Church of England and Ireland who lived in the small village of Brockton that straddled a dusty Dundas Street on the western outskirts of the young City of Toronto. Before the parish was established it was necessary for the worshippers to travel all the way into the city to attend services at St. James's at King and Church streets. With the creation of the new parish, services were initially held in a variety of public places in the neighbourhood. It wasn't until architect Kivas Tully's new building (built with bricks donated by Charles Denison whose famous family was responsible for many of the area's street names) was completed in 1864 that the congregation of St. Ann's, Brockton (still spelled without that final *e*), had its very own church.

Over the years the church was well used and soon became too small for west Toronto's fast-growing population of Church of England supporters. Eventually, it was time for a new edifice. A

Interior of St. Anne's Anglican Church on Gladstone Avenue with some of the works by members of the Group of Seven visible.

design competition was held, and the winner was W. Ford Howland, a prominent Toronto architect. His concept was based on the Byzantine style, a singularly unusual choice for the Toronto of the early 20th century. It's said the architect chose for the new St. Anne's (now there's a final *e*) certain features of St. Sophia in Istanbul. The cornerstone of today's St. Anne's was tapped into place in June 1907.

A key player in the creation of the new church and its remarkable interior decoration was the Reverend Lawrence Skey. He oversaw the construction of the building while holding tight to a dream of making the church's interior one of the finest anywhere in the world. In 1923 Samuel Stewart, one of the parishioners, left a gift of $5,000 to the church, and Skey encouraged the congregation to match the figure. When that was accomplished, he had the money necessary to pursue his dream. Involved in the massive project were artists such as the Group of Seven's Fred Varley and J.E.H. MacDonald and several of their students as well as renowned Canadian sculptors Frances Loring and Florence Wyle. Any attempt to do justice to the interior of St. Anne's is far beyond the scope of this column. But here's an idea. The church often hosts a variety of musical productions, and that's a perfect chance to see and experience this magnificent Toronto landmark that has been acclaimed as both a provincial and federal historic monument. For more information on upcoming performances at St. Anne's, see *www.stannes.on* or phone 416-536-3160.

* * *

Here's an interesting confluence of Toronto transportation anniversary dates. It was on November 16, 1891, that one of Toronto's two Belt Line services began operating. And on November 17, 1894, the other Belt Line service ended. Now in case you're totally confused, Toronto had two distinct Belt Lines. One was a steam train operation, the other a very popular streetcar route. The older of the two services, the one that debuted in 1891, began operating when the horse-drawn streetcars of the privately owned Toronto Railway Company (TRC) began operating the vehicles in both directions on a "belt-shaped" routing using Bloor, Spadina, King, and Sherbourne. To comply with the recently negotiated contract with the city, the TRC began electrifying its various routes (beginning with Church Street in the summer of 1892)

Major infrastructure work is underway on Spadina Avenue in the summer of 1902 as one of the Toronto Railway Company's streetcars on the popular Belt Line trundles by.

and got around to replacing the horse cars on the Belt Line with electric vehicles on December 15 of that year. When the municipally owned Toronto Transportation Company (since 1954 the Toronto Transit Commission) took over the company's city operations in 1921, it retained the Belt Line for a time only to eliminate it in the summer of 1923. To cover the north-south directions, new streetcar lines were established on Sherbourne and Spadina, while the east-west traffic was conveyed on the Bloor and King streetcars.

As for that other Belt Line, it was a pioneer commuter line with many of the same goals as today's GO Transit. The Yonge Loop operated from the old Union Station on the waterfront via tracks in the Don Valley, along a right-of-way between St. Clair and Eglinton avenues (running north of Eglinton just west of today's Avenue Road), then back to the downtown station via tracks west of Dufferin Street. This line (plus a Humber Loop) was established in the spring of 1892 by the Belt Land Company to entice people to purchase land from the company and build homes along the northern fringes of the city. The steam trains and passenger coaches of the Belt Line railway would ease their daily commuters to and from the big city. Unfortunately, the timing was off. Land prices plummeted, and after only 27 months in service the Belt Line railway ceased operations in 1894. Much of the route is now jogging paths and bikeways.

November 16, 2003

Banking on Pizza

Not long after the Town of York came into being in 1793 and the first rudimentary streets began to appear, one of its prominent citizens, Peter MacDougall, Esquire, built for himself a large residence at the northwest corner of Church Street and what was then called Market Street (the former so named because it led to St. James's Cathedral, and the latter called thus because it led to the town market, now the St. Lawrence Market).

Some years later MacDougall's house was converted into a hotel that for many years was the little town's finest. Originally known as Ontario House and, according to the new city's first street directory, located at 2 Market Street, the hostelry's name was changed about 1845 to the Wellington Hotel, no doubt because the street on which it was located had recently been renamed Wellington in honour of Arthur Wellesley, the first Duke of Wellington and the much-revered hero of the Battle of Waterloo.

By the way, the "Iron Duke" was held in such high esteem in Toronto that city officials decided to honour him with a second street, Wellesley, farther uptown. For a while a section of the modern Dundas Street between Bathurst and Ossington was called Arthur perhaps, though not yet verified, as another tribute to the duke.

In 1862 the old Wellington Hotel was demolished and in its place the recently organized Bank of Toronto built a magnificent new head office.

Bank of Toronto building
on the northwest corner
of Wellington and Church
streets, circa 1900.

The Wellington and Church
northwest corner today.

This bank, one of the nation's oldest, had received its charter on March 18, 1855, and after searching the young city (population 41,000) for an appropriate site for its first branch office finally decided on a building at 78 Church Street, opposite the cathedral grounds and between Court and Adelaide streets. A portion of that building still stands.

Just one year short of reaching its 100th birthday, the classic old building on Wellington was demolished in 1961 and a modern banking pavilion was erected in its place. This glass-enclosed structure would become home to a branch of the Toronto-Dominion Bank, the new financial institution that resulted from the February 1, 1955, amalgamation of the Dominion Bank (established 1871) and the Bank of Toronto.

Some years later the Toronto-Dominion Bank abandoned the corner altogether, and before long the former banking pavilion was home to a

143

pizza outlet. Interestingly, nearly a century and a half after the bank first opened at the northwest quadrant of the Church and Wellington intersection, one can still find dough on this ancient corner.

*   *   *

Permit me to go back to the bridge-to-the-Island controversy for a moment. If nothing else, this ongoing debate has given me lots of material for my *Sunday Sun* columns. For instance, when the Toronto Harbour Commission (re-established as the Toronto Port Authority a few years ago) was established in 1911 to oversee the redevelopment of Toronto's badly disjointed waterfront, one of the promises made by the federal government of the day was to build a new bridge to connect the city with Toronto Island. This bridge, to be erected near the foot of Bathurst Street, would be part of a modern vehicular boulevard that would permit traffic to skim along the city's western waterfront, out over the Western Channel, along the Island shoreline, and back to the mainland east of downtown via another bridge across the Eastern Channel. Nothing happened.

In 1935 another attempt was made to connect the city with the Island, this time in the form of a tunnel under the Western Channel. The justification for this "fixed link" was to provide access to and from the new airport proposed for the Hanlan's Point area. The tunnel's construction would also help the labour situation still suffering from the effects of the Great Depression. While a start was made on a tunnel (a large hole on the mainland side was dug), a change in federal governments resulted in the cancellation of the project.

And while the tunnel never materialized, the airport did. To provide vehicle and passenger access to and from what was called Port George VI Island Airport, a new ferry was constructed. In fact, it was nothing more than a steel scow 80 feet long and 30 feet wide and capable of conveying 40 passengers and up to eight cars or trucks. It was propelled by a gasoline-powered winch and a pair of cables affixed to the mainland and Island side of the channel. Activating the winch allowed the ferry to haul itself across the gap. There was a problem, though. If the operator took up the slack without checking the marine traffic using the channel, the rope could easily shear off a sailboat's keel. Not a good thing.

November 23, 2003

Skating on Thin Ice

One of the saddest, most forlorn sights in Toronto has to be old Maple Leaf Gardens at Carlton and Church streets. Once the most boisterous, lively, and exciting place in all of Toronto (and on some nights in all of Canada), the Gardens fell on tough times following the move of the Leafs to Air Canada Centre in late February 1999. Since the abandonment of the Gardens, a variety of ideas have been proposed to help breathe new life into the place, but for reasons I'm not privy to, none was acceptable to the arena's owners.

As for the general public, its ideas on the future of the Gardens range from one extreme to the other. Many people think the building should become a hockey museum, with the millions of dollars necessary for the conversion coming from some unidentified source. Just what would happen to the current Hockey Hall of Fame isn't addressed by those suggesting this course. Others believe the Gardens' time is up and the old place should be put out of its misery. Get rid of it! these people urge. The site is perfect for condo towers and townhouses.

Without a tenant the place continues to deteriorate, but there seems to be a glimmer of hope. Not long ago a new proposal was made public. It seems Maple Leaf Gardens is to be sold to the people who own Loblaws and the place will be converted into one of those ubiquitous big-box superstores.

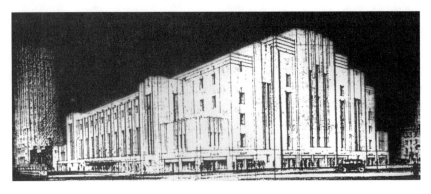

The original look of Toronto's new Maple Leaf Gardens as seen in this early architectural sketch had to be severely altered as money to build it became harder to find.

Most people wince at this thought. Canada's hockey temple converted into a huge food, drug, and clothing emporium? What an awful thought. But, wait, wouldn't a sympathetic conversion of the building into a lively and, yes, even profitable people place, a place that hopefully will retain some of the aura and many of the features of the original Gardens be a better choice than the other option available to the owner? And just what is that other option? Total and complete demolition of the building.

Now before you think I've lost my interest in trying to hang on to what few historically significant buildings we still have in this city, let me point out a fact that most people are unaware of or simply choose to overlook. The Ontario Heritage Act, the province's ultimate set of rules by which a building's future is determined, doesn't provide a mechanism that prevents demolition. It merely supplies a time frame during which the building's future can be negotiated. Sometimes these negotiations are successful. All too often they aren't. Nevertheless, once the prescribed period of time as outlined in the act has lapsed, and as long as the necessary permits for the new project have been approved by the city's planners, the owner has every right to request a demolition permit. And if all the rules have been followed, that permit must be issued.

That's why I think the Loblaws people instead of being assailed should be thanked. The company's plan to renovate, restore, and reuse is one we should embrace. Especially when one considers the alternative afforded under provincial law.

Let me now get down off my soapbox and talk a little about the reason we even have Maple Leaf Gardens, a place many of us are eager to see preserved in the most practical and sympathetic way.

The 1930–31 NHL season was well underway and one thing was painfully obvious to Conn Smythe, the owner of the Toronto Maple Leafs hockey team. His team was just too popular. In addition to the 9,000 or so people who could squeeze into the team's home rink on Mutual Street, there were several thousand others who desperately wanted to spend their good money to see the team play. And with all that extra money Connie could buy better players and attract even more fans. And more fans meant more money. With the Mutual arena bursting at the seams, there was only one answer: the Leafs had to have a new and larger rink.

Smythe was able to interest several prominent Toronto businessmen in his quest. And while most of the money to build the new facility seemed to be in hand, the location was still worrisome. Smythe looked at a piece of Harbour Commission property on the waterfront (interestingly, not far from the Leafs' current home, the Air Canada Centre) as well as the parcel on which the old Knox College on Spadina Avenue north of College is located. Neither alternative was acceptable.

What did interest Smythe, though, was the piece of property on the north side of Carlton Street just east of the brand-new Eaton's College Street store. A deal was struck and on June 1, 1931, steam shovels began

It was in this building, the Labour Temple at 167 Church Street, that the Gardens project was saved when union members agreed to take partial payment in Gardens shares.

excavations for the mammoth new hockey palace. Less than six months later 13,542 fans squeezed into the new Maple Leaf Gardens to watch Chicago beat the Leafs 2–1. Things got better that season, however, and Toronto eventually won the 1931–32 Stanley Cup.

A fascinating and little-known fact about building the Gardens features a rather nondescript building farther down Church Street, a structure whose demolition is imminent. When it was discovered that there was a gap of a few hundred thousand dollars between the amount of money needed to complete the already trimmed-back project and the money Smythe had been able to raise, the project appeared doomed. Then, as a last resort, Smythe's assistant, Frank Selke, a long-time union electrician, approached the various union business managers at a special meeting convened at the Labour Temple just south of the Gardens at 167 Church Street. Would the union members working on the project consider taking 20 percent of their pay in Gardens shares? An agreement meant the Gardens would be completed. But if the unions refused to co-operate, the whole thing was off.

Obviously, the unions agreed to the scheme, and the Gardens hosted its first game on November 12, 1931. And while the Gardens appears to have a new life ahead of it, demolition of the Labour Temple, where the project was rescued, is still in the cards.

November 30, 2003

* The new building on the southeast corner of Church and Shuter streets incorporates the facade of the old Labour Temple. Maple Leaf Gardens is scheduled to reopen in the spring of 2007 as a Great Canadian Superstore complete with displays commemorating the Gardens' storied history.

Take Off, Eh?

December 17, 2003, marks the 100th anniversary of the Wright Brothers' flight at Kitty Hawk, North Carolina. While several efforts were made on that day to get their flying machine off the ground, it was actually the fourth attempt that gave the boys their immortality. That 59-second, 852-foot flight at an altitude of 15 feet is now recognized as the "first sustained manned flight in a controlled gasoline-powered aircraft," and that's what the world celebrates on December 17 each year.

The Wrights conducted their experiments on the lonely sand dunes of North Carolina, so it's not surprising that first-hand reports of this historic happening were few and far between. In fact, it's said that of the thousands of newspapers being published in 1903 only three carried any record of the brothers' historic achievement.

In the highly unlikely chance that Toronto's *Evening Telegram* might have been one of them, I searched each day's copy of that paper for a full week following December 17, 1903, and the best I could come up with was the coverage given to the Dominion Pigeon Fanciers monthly meeting at the Gladstone Hotel on Queen Street West.

Actually, another six years would pass before a heavier-than-air-machine would make an appearance in Toronto. That event occurred in September 1909 when American aviator Charles Willard brought his Curtis biplane, dubbed *The Golden Flier*, to the Scarborough Beach

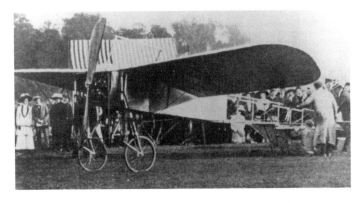

Count Jacques de Lesseps's Blériot XI monoplane, nicknamed *Le Scarabée*, at the First Toronto Aviation Meet held at the Trethewey Farm near Weston, July 8 to 10, 1910. This was the very first powered heavier-than-air craft to fly over the City of Toronto.

amusement park out on Queen Street East. Newspaper advertisements trumpeted that Willard and his flying machine would "sail" from the park to Niagara Falls. And while visitors to the park cheered as the flimsy craft rose from the sandy beach and headed south, the trip was cut short when Willard and his *Flier* crash-landed in the lake. An embarrassed Willard put his wet but undamaged flying machine back into its crate and promptly left town.

The next flying demonstrations held locally took place in mid-July 1910. The eight-day event was staged on the farm of William Trethewey (of Trethewey Road fame) near Weston and was grandly identified as the First Toronto Aviation Meet. The show was so popular that both the Canadian Pacific and the Grand Trunk railways put on special trains to transport the immense crowds. Admission to the show was $1, which included the train ride to and from Union Station.

The stars of these demonstrations were Wright biplanes and Blériot monoplanes flown by such aviation pioneers as William Carruthers, J.G. Stratton, and Ralph Johnstone. But the aviator who stole the show was Count Jacques de Lesseps, the son of Ferdinand de Lesseps, who years earlier had supervised the building of the Suez Canal. Early on the evening of July 13 the count banked his Blériot monoplane away from the Trethewey Farm and headed towards Toronto. As he flew over the city, people gazed skywards to witness the first airplane in history to fly over Toronto.

December 14, 2003

Parkway with a Past

The type of "The Way We Were" column that gets the most attention from my readers involves using an old photograph and asking the question: "Do you know where this is?" Here's another example in that same vein. Examine the accompanying photo closely. Any idea where it is? Here's a hint. The river in the foreground is the Don. And on the east bank, sharp-eyed readers might be able to see a bulldozer doing some grading. And in the background there's a narrow road leading off into the distance. So just where is this and what the heck is going on?

Give up?

The photographer has captured preliminary work being done on the new Don Valley Parkway. The location in this view is near Pottery Road and the future Todmorden Mills Park. That road climbing out of the valley is the Bayview Extension on its way north to the Bayview-Moore intersection. To be even more precise, the hill in the background was once the site of the ill-fated "Bayview Ghost" apartment project and is now blanketed with new houses on streets to be known as True Davidson Drive and Hampton Park Crescent (the former name honouring the lady who served as an East York teacher, reeve, and mayor, and the latter the name of the original "Bayview Ghost" development proposed for this site).

The first phase of the multi-year DVP project began with the construction of the Bloor Street to Eglinton Avenue section. Work commenced in the spring of 1958, and the one-and-a-quarter-mile stretch opened to traffic on August 3, 1961.

Over the next five years other sections opened in the following order: Eglinton to Lawrence, October 31, 1963; the Gardiner/DVP connecting link between Yonge and Bloor streets, November 4, 1964; and Lawrence to Highway 401, November 17, 1966. Since then the DVP has been pushed farther and farther north, with the Sheppard Avenue to Steeles Avenue section (as Highway 404) opening in 1977. The government has proposed that Highway 404 will ultimately connect with Highway 48 near Sutton.

The sounds of flowing water and rustling tree leaves would soon be replaced by the cacophony of cars, trucks, and buses. Any idea where this photo was taken? And when?

That's the recent history of the Don Valley Parkway with a brief look into the future of this important traffic artery and its northern extension. However, as with most supposedly modern concepts, the DVP has an equally interesting past. In fact, the notion of what was originally referred to as a "speedway through the valley of the Don River" can be traced back to the early 1930s.

With the effects of the worldwide Depression worsening, civic officials promoted the construction of a new highway as a way to get men back to work. The route they proposed for the south end of the "speedway" was similar to that followed by today's DVP along the east bank of the river. However, because the phenomenal growth of the city northwards hadn't yet been visualized, engineers agreed that the new "speedway" would curve westerly north of the Prince Edward Viaduct and follow the route of the old railway Belt Line through Moore Park and Mount Pleasant Cemetery with the road's terminus at Mount Pleasant Road and Merton Street then in the northern reaches of the city.

As with most projects of the day, though, money was a problem. In fact, the city looked for civic-minded citizens to donate the land over which the highway would be built. When no one came forward, the idea soon died on the drawing board. Nevertheless, most officials and traffic experts thought the concept was good, and several more attempts were made over the following years to get the "speedway" built. It was even approved by the electorate on the same municipal ballot that gave the go-ahead to the construction of the Yonge Street subway. However, while the creation of the subway began in the fall of 1949, the idea of the "speedway" continued to languish.

Finally, in the early spring of 1958, officials of the newly created Municipality of Metropolitan Toronto announced that a six-lane-wide ribbon of concrete nearly 10 miles in length would be built from Keating Street (now Lake Shore Boulevard East, east of the Don River) through the valley of the Don northwards to connect with the province's new Highway 401. The limited-access highway, to be known as the Don Valley Parkway (the term *speedway* was out), was expected to cost $28 million (it actually cost $40 million) and be completed by 1965. Officials also predicted that at some undetermined time in the future the new Don Valley Parkway would be extended as far north as Lake Simcoe.

Today the Parkway and its Highway 404 extension northwards terminates at Green Lane (Newmarket), 23 miles north of Highway 401.

December 21, 2003

Path Leads to Past

H ere's another of those "Where is this?" photographs. However, since Toronto has only two major rivers, the location should be a lot easier to identify.

Got it?

The river is, of course, the Humber and the view, taken in the fall of 1956, looks east over the river towards an intersection that no longer exists: Lake Shore Boulevard West and Riverside Drive. With the construction of the Frederick G. Gardiner Expressway in the mid to late 1950s, the lower portion of Riverside Drive was rerouted and became part of the South Kingsway. Today there is a South Kingsway connection with the Gardiner.

This photograph is full of interesting details. To the left is the Canadian National railway bridge over the Humber. The tracks are now also used by GO trains on the Lakeshore West route. To the left of centre and on either side of the river are the footings for the new Gardiner Expressway. To accommodate this new highway the hydro towers seen in the photograph, which were constructed early in the 20th century to bring electricity to the city from Niagara Falls, were removed and the wires placed underground. Next is the old Lake Shore Road bridge over the Humber that was badly damaged during Hurricane Hazel in October 1954.

To the extreme right, at the end of the long walkway, is a portion of the ill-starred Palace Pier Dance Hall. At the bottom right is the infamous Edgecliff Tea Rooms, which by the time this photo was taken provided tourist accommodations. However, for most of its early existence the Edgecliff was used as a gambling den. Its location just across the river made it immune to raids by Toronto police, while the few officers on the Etobicoke force with the whole township to patrol were usually too busy to pay much attention to the Edgecliff's customers. Both the Palace Pier and the Edgecliff disappeared long ago, the Pier as a result of a deliberately set fire in January 1963. A condominium tower now sits astride the site. Next to the Edgecliff and just out of the view was Brooker's drive-in restaurant, one of the city's first (if not the first such restaurant) and home of the best 12-inch hot dog anywhere. Many also visited Brooker's for the Lake Ontario submarine races (nudge, nudge, wink, wink).

It's now one of the most congested thoroughfares in Toronto, but when this photo was taken nearly a half-century ago, things were still fairly tranquil. Where is it?

At the top left is Stelco Canada's Swansea Bolt Works, now demolished. The new Windermere-by-the-Lake townhouse and condominium project is quickly taking shape on this once busy industrial site.

On the city side of the bridge (and progressing easterly towards downtown) sharp-eyed readers might be able to pick out a City Service gas station, the Sunnyside Motor Hotel, and the new Seaway Motor Hotel. Still standing next to it at the corner of Windermere Avenue is a Joy gasoline station. This little structure is of particular interest in that it's the last of many that were once found all over the city. Drivers on Lake Shore and visitors to the Sunnyside part of town may have noticed that the building has been moved off its original site to permit soil remediation to take place. After this procedure, the station will be returned to its original location where it will serve some still-to-be-determined use.

On the south side of Lake Shore Boulevard reclamation of the city's western beaches (now Sir Casimir Gzowski Park) continues.

December 28, 2003

Gateway to Toronto

The stretch of Yonge Street shown in the accompanying photograph has been a part of the busy commuter route between Toronto and the smaller communities such as Thornhill, Richmond Hill, and Aurora to the north for almost 200 years. In fact, it wasn't long after Simcoe's Rangers blazed a trail northwards from the Town of York (after 1834 Toronto) through the forest in the late 1790s (a trail that would become part of today's modern Yonge Street) that pioneer settler Lewis Bapp inaugurated a covered wagon service between the town and the Township of Georgina on the shore of Lake Simcoe.

In 1828 George Playter upgraded the service when he began running slightly more comfortable stagecoaches from York to Holland Landing, but with one proviso: weather permitting. Four years later another pioneer transportation entrepreneur arrived on the scene in the form of William Weller. Born in Vermont in 1799, Weller immigrated to Upper Canada (Ontario) and purchased Playter's coach line. He, too, upgraded the Yonge Street service by establishing a regular year-round service. He then went on to initiate additional stagecoach routes throughout the young province, first to Hamilton and Niagara, then easterly to Port Hope, Cobourg (his hometown), and eventually Montreal.

While steam train service that began operating to the western outskirts of Aurora in 1853 put a dent in the patronage of Mr. Weller's

Yonge Street looking south to Centre Avenue, Thornhill, summer 1949. At the bottom of the hill are the entrances to the Ladies' Golf Club of Toronto (east side of Yonge) and the Thornhill Golf Club (west side). In the foreground weeds begin to cover the tracks of a recently abandoned radial streetcar line that in its heyday ran from the city limits all the way to Lake Simcoe. The tracks were removed in 1950. By the way, a special thanks to Bill Sherk (author of *60 Years Behind the Wheel,* Dundurn Group) for helping identify the two cars coming towards the camera in the Thornhill photo. Both are Fords. The first is a 1934 model while the second dates back to 1936.

Yonge Street stagecoach business, there was still enough intercommunity business on Yonge Street to encourage John Thompson to start a stagecoach service between Richmond Hill and Thornhill. He soon expanded this operation by running the coaches all the way down Yonge Street to the bustling capital city. Brightly painted John Thompson stagecoaches pulled by teams of four horses were seen on the streets of Toronto for more than a quarter-century. The trip from Richmond Hill often took as much as three hours and cost the rattled passenger 75 cents for a return ticket.

Progress in the form of electricity, the newest wonder of the age, overtook the Yonge Street stagecoaches in early 1897 when the first electric car of the newly formed Metropolitan Railway made its way from Hogg's Hollow northwards to Richmond Hill. Actually, the inauguration of this electric service didn't go as smoothly as the preceding sentence would indicate. The contract between the operators and York County officials required that service be in place by November 19, 1896. While construction of the line began smoothly enough, the many hills on Yonge Street and the difficulties encountered in placing dozens of wooden poles to support the overhead wires soon became serious impediments. As the deadline approached, it was agreed that the only way to meet the contractual requirements was to substitute real horse power for the electrical kind, at least until the specially welded track, overhead wires, and electric power supply facilities were all in place.

You think we get snow these days? In the "olden days" giant ploughs like this one were frequently called on to clear the tracks for the radial streetcars.

So while the service was up and running as required by the agreement, the first electric "radial" car didn't enter Richmond Hill (passing through Lansing, Willowdale, Newton's Brook, Thornhill, and Langstaff along the way) until February 1 of the following year. They were called "radials" because the plan was to have a collection of these lines radiate out from Toronto to serve various towns surrounding the big city.

Over the years the Yonge Street radial went through several name changes: Metropolitan Railway, Toronto & York Radial Railway, Metropolitan Division, and North Yonge Railways, the first two being privately owned/operated while the third was part of the Toronto Transportation Commission system. At the peak of service the radial cars on this route ran as far north as Jackson's Point and Sutton, serving Bond Lake (where there was a small pleasure ground), Aurora, and Newmarket.

About a year after the Toronto Transportation Commission began operation (September 1, 1921) the southern terminal of the Lake Simcoe radial line was moved to the new Glen Echo loop at the city limits. It was here that many suburban passengers caught the TTC's Peter Witt streetcars and trailers to continue their journey downtown on the extremely busy Yonge line.

Claiming that the North Yonge service was costing the commission too much money, the TTC abandoned the radial line on March 16, 1930, and substituted gas buses. However, public pressure resulted in the councils of North York, Markham, and Vaughan townships and the Town of Richmond Hill authorizing the TTC to re-introduce the electric radial car service, with the townships and town covering the financial shortfall. As a result, just three months after the initial closure, the radial cars were back in business but now only as far north as Richmond Hill.

This line continued until well after the end of the Second World War when serious shortages of electricity throughout the province forced a number of energy conservation measures to be taken. One of these measures was to replace the electric vehicles on two of the TTC's routes with buses. One of the routes was the Spadina streetcar line, the other the North Yonge radial. Conversion of both lines to bus operation took place in mid-October 1948.

Interestingly, while streetcars returned to Spadina in the summer of 1997, the North Yonge radial's demise appears to be more permanent. But who knows for sure?

Just to bring the Toronto–Richmond Hill commuter story up-to-date, GO bus service was introduced in 1972 with GO train operation commencing six years later.

January 4, 2004

Not Plane Sailing

Perhaps I'm being naive, but the seemingly endless saga of whether or not a bridge across the Western Channel to the City Centre Airport should be built prompts the question: "Is it just this so-called fixed link that some are trying to kill, or is it the whole darn airport?"

If the latter is the case, it's a rather interesting change in thinking about what had originally been envisioned as the city's major airport, one that would replace the collection of small private airports scattered in and around the city. After much deliberation, it was decided to locate the new airport at the west end of Toronto Island where it would be close to the business heart of the city. And to take advantage of this feature a vehicle/pedestrian tunnel under the Western Channel would be built using money, about a million dollars' worth, eagerly provided by R.B. Bennett's federal Conservative government.

Construction of the tunnel began even before work on the airport itself was authorized. One reason for this quick start was to try to get men back to work who had been deprived of employment as a result of the ongoing Depression.

However, a fall election saw the Conservatives turfed out and the anti-Toronto Liberals under William Lyon Mackenzie King put in charge. Prodded by Sam McBride (an Island resident and city politician), the King government quickly cancelled the tunnel project, even

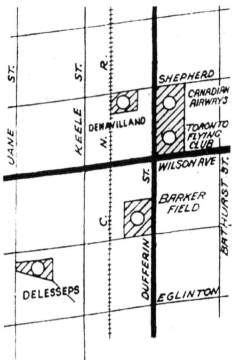

This map showing possible sites for Toronto's proposed civic airport appeared in the "Aviation" column of Toronto's *Evening Telegram* on May 2, 1931.

though substantial money had been spent to do preliminary work at the foot of Bathurst Street (something sound familiar here?).

Officials from the city and the Toronto Harbour Commission (who built and were to operate the facility and who were to become the Toronto Port Authority many years later) tried to change the government's stand but to no avail. Obviously, some other means of crossing the Gap would have to be put in place. The choices were few. Initially, the operators would have to rely on a nameless passenger-carrying barge that was towed back and forth across the 400-foot-wide channel using ropes and winches to do the job. Placed in service soon after the new Port George VI Island Airport (the facility's official name, so chosen in honour of the recent visit of the British monarch to Toronto) opened in 1939, the barge was only a temporary device until a proper connection, such as a bridge, could be put in place.

Actually, the old barge was to remain in service until 1964 when rope power finally gave way to horsepower with the introduction of the diesel-powered *Maple City*. Both the *Maple City* and its backup the *Windmill Point*, the latter vessel purchased from the Ontario Ministry of Transportation in 1985, continue to provide service on one of the shortest voyages in the world. For how much longer? Will there be a bridge? Will there be an airport? Stay tuned.

* * *

While the waterfront site and Malton sites were ultimately chosen for airports, several other locations were also investigated. As seen on the

An artist's conception of the new Terminal One at Pearson International Airport, which opened on April 6, 2004. Our aviation pioneers would have never believed it. (Photo courtesy Greater Toronto Airports Authority)

accompanying map, they include a trio of privately owned airports: the Toronto Flying Club (TFC) field at the northeast corner of Dufferin and Wilson, the Canadian Airways field just north of the TFC airfield, and Barker Field on the west side of Dufferin Street and south of today's Yorkdale Mall. The last only recently had its name changed from Century Airways Airport to Barker Field in honour of Canadian First World War air ace Colonel Billy Barker, who died when his air-craft crashed at Ottawa's airport.

Also shown on the map (though never considered as civic airport sites) are the De Havilland Aircraft (now Bombardier) company air-field and the historic De Lesseps Field (named in honour of Count Jacques de Lesseps, who used this makeshift airport on the farm of W.G. Trethewey to stage the first flight over the city by a heavier-than-air machine during the Toronto Aviation Meet in July 1910). Not shown is Leaside Aerodrome (east of the present Eglinton Avenue East and Laird Drive intersection), which was extremely popular in the early days of local aviation and was closed in 1931 because of encroaching industries.

January 11, 2004

Tracking a Mystery

From 1955 until 1961 I was a student at North Toronto Collegiate Institute, the same school that's currently the subject of often conflicting stories about its future on the Roehampton Avenue site. While at NTCI, I held down a part-time job at Phil Lewis's Redpath Pharmacy, one of those old-fashioned drugstores that one found scattered all over the city in the days before monster drug marts took over.

Phil's store was located on the northwest corner of Eglinton and Redpath avenues and, in fact, is still there, though the prescriptions and drugs were replaced by pancake mix and syrup many years ago when the place became home to the very first Golden Griddle restaurant. During the time I worked at Phil's, I often wondered about the presence of the double set of streetcar tracks in front of the store on Eglinton Avenue. They ran from Yonge Street to Mount Pleasant Road and remained in place even after the connecting curves were removed from the Yonge and Eglinton intersection coincident with the opening of the Yonge subway in early 1954.

But why were they there in the first place? In the years I worked peddling drugs (you know, delivering them on my bicycle) I never saw a streetcar operate over them, nor had any of the many long-time residents of the neighbourhood that I queried when they visited the store.

The mystery was cleared up a few weeks ago when I was scanning the June 17, 1930, edition of the old *Evening Telegram* newspaper,

Eglinton Avenue East looking east to Mount Pleasant Road, June 1930. Toronto Transportation Commission crews are busy laying new streetcar tracks while city crews work on widening the street. Note the old Eglinton Public School to the right of the view.

Same view today. A modern Eglinton school is to the right. The bank building on the northwest corner of the Mount Pleasant Road–Eglinton Avenue intersection is still there, while most of the houses in the earlier view have been replaced by office towers.

looking for something totally unrelated, and came across a brief report entitled "Eglinton Avenue Car Line." Here is that report with my comments in square brackets:

> The TTC, in order to anticipate the district's immediate needs, is laying double tracks on Eglinton Avenue east from Yonge Street to Mount Pleasant Road in conjunction with the widening of the street to 86 feet [Eglinton Avenue was originally a dirt-covered, 66-foot-wide concession road, the fourth, laid out one-and-a-quarter miles or one concession north of St. Clair Avenue]. For months it has been rumored that the TTC has decided that a new cross-town line on Eglinton Avenue from Bathurst to Mount Pleasant Road is necessary. The section now being laid is intended to handle traffic when the new Northern Vocational School [now Northern Secondary School] on Mount Pleasant Road opens next autumn [the new school opened both ahead of schedule and under budget]. Real-estate men in North Toronto welcome the line. One predicted that just as soon as the new Bathurst Street bridge [over Cedarvale Ravine north of St. Clair] and the Eglinton Avenue bridge [over the old Belt Line right-of-way west of Chaplin Crescent] are finished and opened the TTC will establish a streetcar line from St. Clair Avenue up Bathurst and east along Eglinton [to connect with the existing car line on Mount Pleasant Road]. All the district needs for substantial development is the new car line.

Over time the projected development throughout North Toronto materialized. However, that proposed new streetcar line along Eglinton Avenue did not. Toronto Transit Commission records reveal that the tracks were ultimately buried in asphalt in 1959. End of mystery, end of story.

January 18, 2004

Past Waxes Poetic

Another condominium is planned in downtown Toronto. So what else is new? Actually, in this particular case, the phrase should be "so what else is old." That's because as part of this particular project, which will be known as King's Court, the developer has agreed to retain the facade of the old Imperial Bank of Canada frontage at the corner of King and Sherbourne as well as a pair of "ancient" brick houses farther up the street at the Adelaide corner.

In volume 1 of *Robertson's Landmarks of Toronto*, those two houses are identified as having been built, circa 1848, by Paul Bishop, a French-Canadian gentleman whose real surname was L'Eveque. Upon his arrival in Toronto, Monsieur L'Eveque anglicized his surname, becoming Mr. Bishop in the process. He had many trades, including blacksmith and mechanic. And, to quote *Landmarks of Toronto*, he was "one of the best lock-makers in the entire country."

It was Bishop who, using patterns brought to town from Montreal, built the city's first horse-drawn cab for Thornton Blackburn, the city's first cab driver. Incidentally, a site on the north side of Eastern Avenue near the corner of Cherry Street on which Blackburn's residence stood, was the subject of an archaeological dig several years ago during which many interesting household artifacts were uncovered.

A search through successive years of Toronto city directories reveals a multitude of tenants who occupied Bishop's two old buildings

Houses built by Paul Bishop on the south-east corner of Sherbourne and Adelaide streets, 1885. (Photo: Toronto Reference Library)

The same view in 2004.

as either a residence or, in a couple of cases, as a factory. One of the latter was the Edward Hawes Company, manufacturer of Hawes paste wax. The company name appears at the Sherbourne and Adelaide corner in the directories published in the 1930s, and the firm's presence at this address accounts for the painted advertisement on the south wall of the westernmost building. This sign suddenly appeared when an adjacent, and obviously newer structure, was torn down to make way for the new condo. The ad will vanish once again as the new King's Court project rises into the sky.

A portion of advertisement painted on the south wall of the Paul Bishop building.

As a kid, I vaguely remember seeing a product called Hawes Wax, though I don't know if it's still available. Can any readers provide details on this old Toronto company?

By the way, plans call for the two historic buildings built by Paul Bishop to be restored to their grandeur of a century and a half ago and offered for sale.

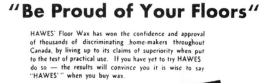

"Be Proud of Your Floors"

HAWES' Floor Wax has won the confidence and approval of thousands of discriminating home-makers throughout Canada, by living up to its claims of superiority when put to the test of practical use. If you have yet to try HAWES do so — the results will convince you it is wise to say "HAWES'" when you buy wax.

Best Known
Fastest Selling

Hawes Wax newspaper ad, 1932.

* * *

For fans of Toronto history some good news. Eric Arthur's book *No Mean City*, which first appeared in 1964 and soon became a bestseller and a landmark publication on the subject of Toronto's architectural history, is available once again. It's been reprinted by University of Toronto Press and contains important revisions by Stephen Otto as well as several new essays by architectural historians. The book continues to be the "Bible" of early Toronto architecture.

January 25, 2004

Fire!

For many years a fragment of old Toronto could be seen rising above the rooftops of several ancient and undistinguished buildings on the west side of Yonge Street, a block or so north of the busy College/Carlton intersection. In fact, in more recent times there were frequent calls for the demolition of this rickety old structure, lest it collapse and do harm to passersby. It sure looked as if the clock tower of Fire Hall Number 3 was doomed.

Today, thanks to concerned citizens who became passionate about keeping the tower, the structure has been given a new lease on life, as has the rest of the site, with new shops at street level and apartments and offices above.

What makes this old landmark so interesting is the fact that it's such an obvious reminder of the earliest days of firefighting in Toronto, a service that many of us in this modern day and age take for granted except, of course, when we need it.

While Toronto was still a small town, firefighting efforts were provided by the citizens themselves, who upon being alerted to a fire, either by shouts for help or by the ringing of the bell in the tower of St. James's Cathedral, formed a double line from the bay or cistern nearest the conflagration and passed full buckets of water up one side and empty ones down the other. In fact, it wasn't until 1826 that a volunteer fire brigade was organized that resulted in some semblance

170

of order being given to what had often become chaotic firefighting efforts.

It was also about that time that the community purchased its first piece of firefighting equipment — a hand-operated pumper called the *York*. This rudimentary piece of apparatus, which was hauled to the fire scene by a group of eager firemen, was housed in the town's first and, for many years, only fire hall — a two-storey building on the west side of Church Street between Court and Adelaide.

To supply water for the new pumper to pump, what was known as the "puncheon system" was introduced. This system featured a few enterprising citizens outfitting horse-drawn carts with large barrels capable of holding 60 to 80 gallons of water. When an alarm was sounded, these people rushed their rigs to the site of the fire where volunteers fed the *York* with water from the barrels. The first to appear on the scene was awarded a payment equivalent to $3, with the second, third, and fourth arrivals getting $2, $1, and 50 cents respectively. The desire to be first at the scene often resulted in violent races through the town and participating carters arriving with half-full barrels.

While the water arrived at the fire in horse-drawn carts, the fire apparatus continued to be propelled by out-of-breath firemen. That all changed in the early 1860s when real horsepower was introduced, and for the next few decades the sight of horse-drawn, smoke-belching steam

Fire Hall Number 3 on Yonge Street as it looked not long after it was closed in June 1929.

A victim of time and neglect, the clock tower of old Number 3 Fire Hall was recently restored thanks to Joe Bogoroch, a Toronto businessman with a sense of history. Heritage Toronto recognized Mr. Bogoroch for his efforts at a Heritage Awards Evening.

pumpers careering through city streets to help quell a blaze was something not soon forgotten.

It wasn't long after the horses were introduced that city fathers decided to build two more fire halls to serve the city that now had a population in excess of 50,000. One of these new halls was on Portland Street at the west end of the city, and the other was on the west side of Yonge Street between Grosvernor and Grenville. They would supplement the existing fire halls, the original at Church and Court streets in the old part of town and a second at Bay and Temperance streets.

The Grosvenor Street fire hall replaced the old Yonge Street hall, which was then closed. The new hall retained the number 3, but upon amalgamation of the various fire departments throughout Metro Toronto in 1998 the Grosvenor hall was renumbered 314.

The new Yonge Street fire hall was completed in 1870 and served the area for more than a half-century. When firefighters moved around the corner into the new Grosvenor Street hall in the late 1920s, old Number 3 sat vacant for many years before being occupied by a succession of different tenants: a used-car dealer, a tire dealer, and lastly, the St. Charles Tavern (remember its motto, "Meet me under the clock"?).

In recent years the future looked bleak for the fire hall's landmark clock tower. However, Toronto businessman Joe Bogoroch, working with Climans, Green, Liang Architects, stepped in and saved the day.

So next time you're in the Yonge-Carlton-College neighbourhood, pause, look up, set your watch, and say a quiet thank-you to Mr. Bogoroch.

February 1, 2004

March of Time

A familiar sight to many thousands of motorists who travel the busy stretch of Avenue Road north of St. Clair Avenue each workday is the clock tower of Upper Canada College. This is actually the second such structure to stand on the site, the original having been replaced when it was found to be structurally unsafe. The new tower mimics the original.

On the subject of Upper Canada College, it was on May 2, 1829, that Sir John Colborne, who had just been appointed lieutenant governor of the Province of Upper Canada (after 1867, Ontario), placed the following notice in an edition of the local newspaper: "Minor College — Sealed tenders for erecting a school-house and four dwelling houses will be received on the first Monday of June next. Plans, elevations and specifications may be seen after the 12th instant on application to the Honourable George Markland, from whom further information may be received."

Since his arrival, Colborne had been under great pressure from a few of York's (after 1834, Toronto) most influential citizens to ensure that the young community became the site of a full-fledged university. However, the new lieutenant governor had something else in mind. Instead of a university, the establishment of which he felt was premature in a community of fewer than 4,000 people, he promoted the creation of an educational facility that would be a stepping stone and ultimate feeder to the proposed university. (That new university, originally known as King's College, would welcome its first students in 1843. It would be reorganized and renamed the University of Toronto six years later.)

It is said that Colborne's desire to create a preparatory institution was prompted by the fact that in his capacity as lieutenant governor of the Isle of Guernsey, a position he held prior to being reassigned to Upper Canada, Colborne was instrumental in the revival of Elizabeth College, an ancient teaching facility that had been established in 1563 and had fallen on hard times. (By the way, it was Colborne who came up with the name of Sarnia for that western Ontario city. Sarnia was the Roman word for Guernsey. Fascinating stuff, eh?)

While the buildings to house Colborne's new school were taking shape near the northwest corner of King and Simcoe streets, inaugural classes were held in an existing building at the corner of the modern-day Lombard and Jarvis streets. By January 1831 the new buildings were ready, and soon the staff and pupils moved in. The school remained in its downtown location for 60 years, eventually moving to a remote site in suburban Deer Park (so named because of the many deer that roamed the area).

A prominent feature of the new school was its clock tower, which soon became an area landmark. In the late 1950s engineers detected major problems in the structure, so it had to be replaced. The current tower, a duplicate of the original, is officially known as the Rogers Tower in recognition of donations made by several members of the Rogers family, including Ted Rogers, Jr., a graduate of UCC, and his mother, Velma Rogers Graham.

While we're on the subject of Avenue Road, have you ever wondered how the street got its rather unusual name? Avenue Road — it's like Street Avenue, Road Street, or some similar combination. Actually, there are two possibilities for the origin of the name. I'll offer both and you decide which one sounds most probable.

The original name of today's University Avenue was College Avenue because it ran from Queen Street north to King's College, a structure that stood where the provincial Parliament Buildings stand today. Over the years the term College Avenue was shortened to simply "the Avenue." As a result, years later when the Avenue was extended north of Bloor, the new thoroughfare was often referred to as the road to the Avenue or ... Avenue Road.

In the 1870s a group of land developers from England were scouting the district in and around today's Bathurst and St. Clair intersection for

Avenue Road looking north over St. Clair Avenue in 1935. Numerous trees overhanging the narrow street block the view of Upper Canada College and its landmark clock tower.

The same view in 2004. Almost all of the beautiful old houses are gone, and the street has been widened considerably. As a result, the college and tower are now clearly visible in the centre background.

new housing sites. Late in the day the group made its way along the dusty Third Concession Road (St. Clair) to Yonge, which they would follow to downtown Toronto and their hotel. As the men straggled eastwards, and with Yonge Street still far in the distance, one of the visitors turned to another and remarked, "You know, we oughta 'ave a new road here."

Take your pick. I know which one I like.

*   *   *

I was sorry to hear of the recent passing of Jack Jones, the former chief engineer for the Toronto Harbour Commission. I met Jack on many occasions, and we often chatted about the city's waterfront and the Island. He had numerous ideas on how he would improve its appearance and make them, as he would say, more people friendly. Readers may recall that I recently wrote about one of Jack's ideas to improve access to the Island Airport. He suggested creating a new Western Gap south of the airport. Then, by filling in the present Gap, the airport would become part of the mainland. Voilà, a multimillion-dollar bridge is no longer necessary. And the new Gap prevents vehicles from ever getting onto the Island proper.

Another thing Jack suggested was a pedestrian-only tunnel from the foot of Bathurst to the airport. The tunnel would be fitted out from end to end with a travelling walkway similar to that out at Lester B. Pearson International Airport. The present airport ferry would be placed on standby, ready if and when needed for deliveries and emergencies.

I liked chatting with Jack.

February 22, 2004

Fuel for Thought

In the previous column I featured "then and now" views of Avenue Road looking north over St. Clair Avenue. The photos were snapped (do you snap a picture with a digital camera?) nearly 70 years apart, the older one in 1935 and the more modern one in 2004.

What a surprise it was then to find in the mail after the column first appeared a packet of old photographs taken by reader Clifford Crawford. Among the shots was a view taken from the same intersection as the "then" view in the aforementioned column, though this time the picture shows, among other landmarks, the newly opened Imperial Oil Building at 111 St. Clair Avenue West. In the letter that accompanied the photos, Clifford explained that since his arrival in Toronto in June 1955 he had taken numerous views in and around his adopted city. One day, while sorting through his collection, he came across a few that he thought I might be able to make use of as I, as he says in his letter, "continue to record the development of this great city so many of us appreciate."

In acknowledgment of Clifford's request, I offer one of his photos here. Thanks, Cliff.

When Clifford aimed his camera east along St. Clair Avenue from the Avenue Road corner, the most prominent feature in his viewfinder was the new Imperial Oil head office building that had only recently opened on the south side of the street at number 111. The cornerstone

St. Clair Avenue looking east from Avenue Road, circa 1957. Prominent in this view is the newly constructed Imperial Oil Building that towers over the little Deer Park United Church. Next to it, at the southeast corner of St. Clair Avenue and Avenue Road, is the Deaconess House of the United Church of Canada. Some may remember when this building was home to Blue Cross. Moving out of the view is one of the Toronto Transit Commission's Presidents' Conference Committee (PCC) Streamliner streetcars.

of this structure was laid on September 8, 1955 (interestingly, just days after my classic turquoise-and-white Pontiac Laurentian two-door hardtop rolled off the assembly line at General Motors in Oshawa).

Imperial Oil Company Limited was established in 1880, following the amalgamation of 16 southwestern Ontario refiners who pooled their resources to create a new company to find, produce, refine, and distribute a variety of petroleum products throughout Canada. The company's first head office was located in London, Ontario. Early in the 20th century both automobiles, and the need for petroleum products to power them, had become important realities of Canadian life. In fact, now rather than simply getting rid of what had for years been a refinery by-product, gasoline had become a saleable commodity. In 1907, recognizing this development, Imperial Oil opened the nation's first service station, a rudimentary facility by today's standards, adjacent to its Vancouver warehouse.

As the company grew, so, too, did the need for more office space. In Toronto the company moved into the former Toronto Railway Company building (the privately owned predecessor of the Toronto Transit Commission) at the northwest corner of King and Church streets. However, by the early 1950s it was obvious that even more space was required. This led to the construction of a new 22-storey office tower in the Deer Park section of the city.

Designed by the prominent Canadian architectural firm of Mathers and Haldenby, the 295-foot-high structure was, at the time, the tallest all-welded steel frame building in the world. It also had the distinction of being the "highest" building in the country for several years. That's because while the city's "tallest" building of the day, the Bank of Commerce (now Commerce Court North) on King Street

The same view in 2004. The Imperial Oil Building and the church are still there, while the Deaconess House has been replaced by the Ministry of the Environment Building. And the once ubiquitous PCCs have been supplanted all over town by modern Canadian Light Rail Vehicles.

West, soared 34 stories or 477 feet above street level, the new Imperial Oil Building was erected on the escarpment at the north end of the city. That fact gave the new building a height advantage of 74 feet over the bank. Staff moved into the city's new skyscraper on April 22, 1957.

Next to the Imperial Oil Building is the pretty little Deer Park United Church. Its predecessor, Deer Park Presbyterian (the United Church of Canada came into being in 1925), was on the north side of St. Clair Avenue, just west of the Yonge corner. It was opened in 1888. The cornerstones of the present church (there are two, since the one from the original church was incorporated into the new) were laid in 1911.

At the extreme right of the view is the United Church of Canada's Deaconess House, where women were trained in a variety of non-ministerial endeavours. It was also erected in 1911 and served the church until 1943. It was then used by the military, and in its later years it was the home of Blue Cross. After the old building was demolished, the Ministry of the Environment Building (where I worked for nearly 10 years) was erected in its place.

February 29, 2004

Building on the Past

Accompanying this column, I offer another old photograph snapped by Clifford Crawford. This one shows the view looking north on Bay Street across Queen, circa 1957. I went to the same location and megapixeled (*snapped* seems like such an old-fashioned word when using a digital camera) the same view as it appears in 2004.

In the old photo we see part of Manning Chambers, an early office building owned by and named for Alexander Manning, who served as mayor of Toronto on two separate occasions (1873 and 1885). Manning was a successful real-estate entrepreneur and the person for whom Manning Avenue in west-central Toronto is named.

To the right of the view is a portion of the Toronto City Hall of the day. One of the best-loved buildings in the city (except perhaps by those who discover their fate in the provincial law courts found inside), the structure was officially opened in September 1899 and has been the subject of demolition talk on more than one occasion. In recent years values have changed and the old building now stands proudly at the top of Bay Street, a monumental icon from Toronto's past. Now if we could just find a better use for the "Old" City Hall.

In the middle distance of the old photo, looking like something out of a guide to ancient Italian landmarks, is a building that never really had a chance. Known as the Registry Office, it was intended to be the repository for all city land titles and deeds. The idea was that documents for properties east of Yonge Street would be stored in facilities located in the east side of the building, while similar documents for properties west of Yonge would be housed in the west side of the building. The imposing structure was to be just one of several government buildings located in a Civic Square that was proposed in 1911 by a group known as the Civic Improvement Committee. The square would front on Queen Street opposite a new north-south thoroughfare to be known as Federal Avenue. This avenue would connect Front Street, opposite the main entrance to the new Union Station, with Queen, with its vista focused on the proposed Civic Square. Other components of the square were the University Avenue Armouries (demolished in 1963) as well as Osgoode Hall and today's "Old" City Hall, all of which were already in place.

Like many other grand schemes in Toronto's history (witness the plethora of strategies put forward over the years to enhance the city's waterfront or the aborted plan to hold a world's fair in

Bay Street looking north over Queen Street, circa 1957. Manning Chambers is to the left of the view, and a portion of "Old" City Hall is to the right. The impressive structure in the distance is the Registry Building.

The same view in 2004. Both Manning Chambers and the Registry Building are gone, but "Old" City Hall lives on. (Photo: Yarmila Filey)

Toronto in honour of Canada's centennial), the Civic Square of 1911, as well as an equally grandiose proposal put forward in 1929, never got off the drawing board. Except that is for the Registry Building, which over time found itself passed by, standing alone on Albert Street in one of the city's shabbiest neighbourhoods.

With the later development of a new City Hall, which itself took years to come to fruition, the still stately Registry Building was deemed an obstruction. Officials flirted with the idea of moving the structure out of the way to a place of prominence, somewhere, anywhere. But again, nothing happened. The west tower of "New" City Hall now stands on the site.

* * *

In March 1929, 75 years ago as I write this column, one of Toronto's most famous restaurants and reception halls, the Arcadian Court in the Hudson's Bay store at Queen and Bay streets, opened to the public. A press release issued by the building's original owner, the Robert Simpson Company (which was purchased by The Bay in 1978), boasted that the Arcadian Court was the largest department store restaurant in the world. What the release didn't state was the reason for spending thousands of dollars to create a huge restaurant that would have a seating capacity of nearly 1,300 and occupy two entire floors. In a subsequent interview Charles Luther Burton, who became president of Simpson's in 1929, confessed that the new restaurant was developed in direct response to the competitive reception and dining facilities that would be found in the soon-to-open Royal York Hotel and Eaton's College Street store.

As for the unusual name of the new restaurant, that was the creation of Mrs. N.R. McCullough, who wrote advertising copy for the department store. After he selected a "Grecian" decor for the new dining room, Burton requested that the advertising people come up with a name in keeping with the theme. Mrs. McCullough rose to the challenge and after examining Greek mythology and poetry eventually came across a poem in which a nomadic tribe inhabited a place called Arcady in the Peloponnesian Islands. They loved peace, beauty, and flowers. Burton wanted his new restaurant to embody "peace and beauty among the flowers."

And while the name Arcady was close, it didn't sound quite right. The letters were juggled and a few added as was the term *Court*. Finally they had it. The new restaurant would be called Arcadian Court.

March 7, 2004

The Iceman Cometh

One of my favourite television shows is *The Honeymooners*, a series about the working-class Kramdens starring Jackie Gleason, Audrey Meadows, Art Carney, and Joyce Randolph that first appeared on our family's black-and-white Admiral back in 1955 (coincidentally the same year my classic Pontiac Laurentian two-door hardtop rolled off the General Motors assembly line in Oshawa). Better than a lot of the so-called hit comedy programs of today, *The Honeymooners* can be seen each Sunday on the Comedy Channel, or you can buy it on DVD.

One of the few appliances seen in Alice Kramden's kitchen is an icebox. I wonder how many readers remember when iceboxes were the norm in Toronto and only the well-to-do had a new-fangled electric refrigerator.

While the icebox was certainly easy on the electrical bill, that benefit was more than offset by the inconvenience of always needing a large chunk of ice in the upper chamber so the thing could work. That, plus having to remember to empty the drip pan under the icebox to avoid a flood. Forgetting to do either could turn this so-called convenience into a real inconvenience.

I can vaguely remember the iceman when he cameth down our street. To make sure he knew that you needed ice, a small card was placed in the window. Seeing the card, the iceman would then use a pick to carve a manageable block from the huge blocks transported in

"Harvesting" ice on the Humber River. The structure in the background is the Grand Trunk Railway (now Canadian National Railways) bridge over the river not far from the Weston Golf and Country Club.

Horse-drawn sleigh delivering ice, circa 1930. (Photo: City of Toronto Archives)

the back of his well-insulated wagon. Then, using scissor-like tongs, he'd transfer the block of ice from the wagon into the old icebox.

In the very early days some ice was "harvested" from the frozen Humber River in a manner shown in the accompanying photograph. But as the demand increased, a larger source of ice became necessary and it was then that eyes turned northwards to the frozen waters of Lake Simcoe.

One of the first firms to begin harvesting ice from the lake was the Springwater Ice Company. In 1876 it was acquired by Australian-born James Fairhead, who had been educated in England and who at the age of 21 moved to Canada where he took up residence in the Toronto suburb of Yorkville. For a time Fairhead operated a brickyard in North Toronto before relocating farther north to the small Lake Simcoe community of Lefroy where he purchased the Springwater Ice Company. Fairhead soon changed the establishment's name to Lake Simcoe Ice & Fuel Limited, and it wasn't long before his firm became the major supplier of ice to homes in the Toronto area.

Advertisement for Lake Simcoe Ice & Fuel that appeared in 1931, the same year company founder James Fairhead died.

In 1894 Fairhead acquired several competing companies harvesting ice from the lake, including the well-known Belle Ewart Ice Company, another prominent supplier of ice to homes and businesses in the Toronto area.

James Fairhead passed away on February 3, 1931, at the age of 81 and is buried in Mount Pleasant Cemetery.

Oh, just in case you were wondering, the process of harvesting ice from the lake went like this. Once the ice reached a thickness of at least 12 inches, ploughs were used to clear away the snow while, at the same time, scoring the surface of the ice. Crews, using huge saws, would then cut the surface into large blocks called "rafts" that another crew would lug onshore. Still another crew would carve the rafts into smaller, more manageable 22-inch-by-32-inch blocks, which were then stored in large icehouses scattered along the shoreline.

That was the hard part. Moving the product to the big city to the south was a relatively easy task thanks to the presence of a nearby rail line that had been in use when lumbering was a major industry in the area some years before. Once in the city, ice deliveries were done using the company's 25 to 30 horse-drawn wagons.

It was sometime around 1914 that city health officials deemed that lake ice was no longer acceptable for domestic use. It was then that the company began manufacturing ice in a factory on Dupont Street.

March 14, 2004

Subway Sandwich

March 2004 marks the golden anniversary of the opening of Canada's first subway. It was at precisely 11:50 a.m., Tuesday, March 30, 1954, that the first train went into service on the Toronto Transit Commission's new 4.6-mile-long, 12-station Yonge line. Jam-packed with VIPs and invited guests (the general public had to wait until 1:30 p.m. to give the line a try), the eight-car train "rocketed" nonstop from Eglinton (the north terminal) to Union (the south end of the line) in just a dozen minutes. The event was the culmination of numerous attempts over the decades to ease the traffic chaos that had enveloped the city's main street, an untenable situation that was quite literally strangling the downtown core.

Several of the earlier proposals to construct a "tube" (as subways were called in the early 1900s, a "subway" being a vehicle underpass under railway tracks) in Toronto have been described in detail in previous columns. However, I recently came across a proposal I had never seen before that proves to be much earlier than any of the others. In fact, the 20th century was only nine years old when James Hales, a little-known city alderman representing Ward 2, requested that the city engineer of the day, Charles Rust, prepare a report on the feasibility and costs associated with the construction of not one but a trio of "underground railways" (another term from the past denoting the present word *subway*). The routes would be under Yonge from Front Street to the railway tracks (at

An artist's interpretation of the 1931 Yonge Street "streetcar" subway, one of many proposals that never went any further than the drawing board.

the former Canadian Pacific Railway North Toronto Station, now a liquor store, near Summerhill Avenue); under Queen from Roncesvalles Avenue to the city's east limits (approximately Balsam Avenue in the Beach area); and under King also from Roncesvalles on the west to the Don River.

Rust was very thorough when compiling his report and based his figures on recently completed projects in New York City, Philadelphia, and Boston. He concluded that the cost of constructing the 15.5 miles of tubes under the three major city thoroughfares — Yonge, Queen, and King, as suggested by Alderman Hales — would cost the city approximately $23 million or almost $1.5 million per mile. (For comparison purposes, the construction-only cost of the original 4.6-mile Yonge subway was $14.5 million per mile, while the four-mile Sheppard subway that opened in late 2002 was close to $250 million per mile.)

By the late 1940s, vehicular traffic in the downtown core had increased to such an extent that the Yonge streetcars, such as this one at the Yonge and Richmond intersection, operated at a crawl. A new subway under the street would speed things up.

Rust went on to say in his report that with a city population of only 300,000, taxpayers couldn't afford such a massive expenditure. He recommended that the idea be revisited when the population reached a million, something that didn't happen until the City of Toronto joined with the surrounding communities to form Metropolitan Toronto. And that happened exactly three months before the Yonge line opened in March 1954.

March 21, 2004

Seeking Asylum

L ocated within the historic South St. Lawrence Market at Front and Jarvis streets is the Market Gallery. Established in 1979 by the City of Toronto's Culture Division, this unique facility employs rare old maps, meticulously preserved drawings and photographs, and one-of-a-kind artifacts in exhibitions that give citizens and visitors to Toronto a look at the city that used to be.

One of the more interesting exhibitions featured at the gallery was entitled *The Provincial Asylums in Toronto and Mimico: Reflections on Social and Architectural History*. The history of mental health treatment practices is for many people both a fascinating yet uncomfortable subject. According to Dr. Geoffrey Reaume and John Court, co-curators of the exhibit, in Toronto's earliest years those unfortunates afflicted with what we now call mental illness were simply put somewhere "out of the way." Usually, the local jail would suffice where they would be left to languish until death put them out of their misery. Some of the mentally unsound would be sent to the countryside to board with the lowest bidder in a kind of "out of sight, out of mind" approach. Others were deported, leaving someone else to look after matters.

It wasn't until 1839 that provincial authorities got around to passing a law authorizing the establishment of a permanent "insane asylum." However, another two years would pass before even a "temporary"

Artist W.J. Thomson's 1890 watercolour of the Provincial Asylum on Queen Street West. (Courtesy of the Centre for Addiction and Mental Health Archives)

The Provincial Asylum's infirmary ward, circa 1910. (Courtesy of the Centre for Addiction and Mental Health Archives)

facility was made available while that permanent insane asylum would have to wait until 1850. In that year the Provincial Asylum, located in an almost pastoral setting on the Garrison Common several miles west of the city, took in its first patients.

Treatment at 999 Queen Street West during the asylum's first half-century of operations consisted primarily of physical labour and recreation, techniques that were strongly advocated by the asylum's first two superintendents, Doctors Joseph Workman and Daniel Clark. With the appointment of Dr. C.K. Clarke in 1905 a new approach to treatment was introduced. Classification based on patients' diagnoses became the norm, followed by a period when physical intervention (electro-convulsive treatment, lobotomy, injections) was given preference. That was followed in the 1950s by pharmaceutical medication options and the de-institutionalization of patients. These techniques continue.

In the mid-1970s the provincial government of the day decided that the building that had become known as "999" was a symbol of all that was wrong in the treatment of the mentally ill, even though the institution had, in fact, been the site of some of the civilized world's most innovative and responsible treatment practices. Pressure to retain all or portions of architect John Howard's landmark structure were to no avail and the building was demolished. Today the Queen Street Mental Health Centre occupies the site.

The Market Gallery, open Wednesday to Friday from 10:00 a.m. to 4:00 p.m., Saturday from 9:00 a.m. to 4:00 p.m., and Sunday from noon to 4:00 p.m., is situated in the council chamber of a building that served as City Hall from 1845 to 1899. Admission is always free. For more information call 416-392-7604 or visit *www.stlawrencemarket.com/gallery*.

April 4, 2004

Selfless Service

The skies over Toronto on June 7, 1933, were heavy all morning. When the storm finally struck at about noon, it was violent with plenty of rain and lightning. During the half-hour or so that the tempest raged, the fire department's communications centre was inundated with calls describing lightning strikes all over the city, most minor, a few more serious. Then, just as the storm was subsiding, an alarm came in reporting that a bolt of lightning had struck the dome of Our Lady of Lourdes Church on the west side of Sherbourne Street, just north of Wellesley. Smoke and flames were soon visible and a call went out for help. Within minutes firefighters from both the No. 10 Yorkville and No. 11 Rose Avenue halls were on the scene.

To get at the flames it was necessary to access the lofty dome about 100 feet above ground level. Since the longest extension ladder the firefighters had at their disposal was only about 80 feet long, it became necessary for the men to attack the flames from an extremely precarious and difficult position atop the ladder. The rain was now coming down in torrents, and a strong wind buffeted the crew as it aimed a heavy rubber hose at the blaze. Suddenly, and without warning, the wooden ladder snapped and four of the firefighters tumbled earthwards. Three of them, firefighters Frank Coakwell (who went on to become the city's fire chief from 1962 to 1968), Garfield O'Brien, and William Hughes, hit some nearby electrical

This award-winning photograph by the *Evening Telegram* newspaper's Albert Van captured firefighter Robert Calhoun (second from left) falling to his death while fighting the Our Lady of Lourdes Church fire on June 7, 1933.

wires, an action that helped break their fall. Robert Calhoun, who had served on the force for 17 years, wasn't quite so fortunate. As he plummeted towards the pavement, he was impaled by a jagged fragment of the ladder. The 40-year-old firefighter then hit the ground with a sickening thud. Others came to his aid, but it was too late. Calhoun's lifeless body was taken by ambulance to Wellesley Hospital just down the street, where he was declared dead.

The city went into mourning. Several days later a private service was held at the firefighter's 64 Balfour Avenue residence, attended by his widow, his five children, and his brother, John (who died on duty fighting a house fire 24 years later). Afterwards, Calhoun's flag-draped casket was transported to Mount Pleasant Cemetery on the back of one of the department's fire trucks. In the procession were more than 150 of his comrades.

Part of the inscription on the headstone, which includes the names of his wife and one of his sons, is unusual. Instead of the word *Died*, the word *Killed* appears.

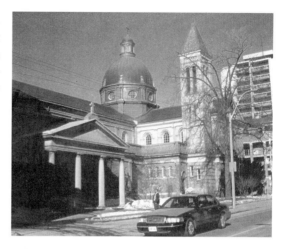

In March 2003 the Our Lady of Lourdes Church's dome is still the building's most obvious architectural feature.

Robert Calhoun's final resting place in Mount Pleasant Cemetery.

Stories about Robert Calhoun and other Ontario firefighters killed in the line of duty are recorded in Robert Kirkpatrick's book *Their Last Alarm* (General Store Publishing House).

April 11, 2004

Toronto's 1904 Inferno

In April 2004 the very heart of Toronto was devastated by a fire that remains to this day the worst in the city's 200-plus-year history. Erupting shortly after 8:00 p.m. in the four-storey E & S Currie Neckwear factory at 58–60 Wellington Street West, what might have been an easily controllable blaze soon erupted into an inferno. By the time it was brought under control more than 10 hours later, it ravaged nearly 20 acres in the city's downtown.

Starting near the northwest corner of Wellington and Bay, the flames, fanned by a cold wind from the northwest, leaped from structure to structure. The low water pressure that was available at hydrants, in combination with buildings constructed using flammable wooden joists and beams and filled with highly combustible materials, gave the fire a head start. Narrow city streets and lanes did little to slow the fiery advance.

By now firefighters from all 15 city fire halls, as well as men and equipment from some outlying communities such as Kew Beach, Toronto Junction, and East Toronto, were responding to the urgent call for help. Also responding were men and equipment from fire halls in London, Hamilton, Brampton, Niagara Falls, and Buffalo. Although the intentions of these out-of-towners were honourable, their assistance arrived too late in most cases.

The fire resulted in the destruction of nearly 140 businesses located in more than 100 buildings in an area centred on Bay and Front

Bay Street looking north from near Wellington Street, April 20, 1904. Note the clock tower of today's "Old" City Hall in the distance. The fire erupted in a building just out of the view to the left. Inset: A similar view, 100 years later, in 2004. Although all has changed, the tower still looks down on the passing scene.

streets and reaching west past York, north to just south of King, east almost to Yonge, and south to the south side of the Esplanade. Estimates of damage exceeded $100 million in 1904 dollars.

Many firefighters were injured in the conflagration, the most serious being Fire Chief Thompson, who suffered a broken leg after sliding down a rope from the fourth floor of a burning building. There were no deaths. However, a fatality did occur several days after the fire when John Croft, a citizen contracted to level the ruins of a structure on Wellington Street, had a charge explode in his face. He died a short time later.

A newspaper account published on the first anniversary of the fire stated embers were still smouldering in the ruins of buildings that occupied the site of today's Union Station.

April 18, 2004

Walking the Plank Road

Although not as old as either the original Dundas Street (today's Queen Street west as far as Ossington, Ossington north to Dundas, then Dundas Street west to London, Ontario) or Yonge Street (old waterfront just south of Front Street, north as far as the road's junction with the Holland River), Weston Road, too, has a fascinating history. It was originally built as a corduroy road connecting the northwestern outskirts of Toronto with the small but busy community of Weston, which at the time straddled both the east and west banks of the Humber River in the vicinity of today's Lawrence Avenue West. The road was used extensively by farmers and others conveying a variety of goods to markets in the young city of Toronto.

The term *corduroy* came from the fact that the logs that were used to create a surface over soft mud, swamp, and other impassible surfaces were cut in half longitude-wise and laid transversely across the track. The roadway so constructed had a ribbed appearance and looked like large pieces of corduroy fabric. Incidentally, the word *corduroy* is a variation of the French term *cord du roi*, a material with a corded appearance that was worn by royalty while hunting.

In the early 1840s traffic had increased sufficiently to justify improving the road surface, and John Grubbe, who had been a successful builder of plank roads in Scotland, obtained government authority to make such improvements. Historical records indicate that

196

Looking north on Weston Road (Main Street) towards the Lawrence Avenue intersection, circa 1900.

A similar view in 2004.

Grubbe and his workers used nearly 2.25-million feet of pine planking, at $4 per thousand feet, to build what became known as the Weston Plank Road. The road ultimately connected the Toronto suburbs with Weston, Thistletown, Claireville and, eventually, Coleraine, a tiny settlement north of Brampton.

Although tolls were charged to use the road, business was never sufficiently high enough to cover the ongoing costs of repairing and replacing the numerous planks that rotted out or were badly damaged by the heavily laden wheeled vehicles. Potholes are not new.

Eventually, the Weston Plank Road was turned over to the county for maintenance. The tolls remained in place, and for a long time toll gates could be found at both the north and south ends of Weston where a five-cent charge was levied. Just before the turn of the century the majority of tolls were abolished throughout the province, never to return many believed.

Visible in the old photograph is the track on which the streetcars of the privately owned Toronto Suburban Street Railway operated. Incorporated in 1894, the line ran from Keele and Dundas streets north on Keele over St. Clair, continued north on Weston Road to King Street, then Church Street in the Village of Weston.

On October 10, 1914, the line was officially opened to Woodbridge with hourly service to and from the Junction via Weston's Main Street (now Weston Road) from 7:00 a.m. until midnight, using large 48-passenger cars. The one-way fare was a dime.

The Weston-to-Woodbridge part of the line was terminated in May 1926, by which time the southern portion was being operated by the TTC under a contract from both the Township of York and Weston, which had purchased the transportation system's assets through their jurisdictions. Electric streetcars continued until replaced by buses (initially, gasoline-powered followed in 1948 by new electric trolley coaches that in turn were laid low by diesel buses more recently).

April 25, 2004

They Shoot, They Score!

Frederick Arthur Stanley was what we would call today a real hockey nut. In fact, history records that he was so taken with the game during his stay in Canada where he served as the young nation's sixth governor general that he decided to donate what he himself described as a "challenge cup" to the best amateur team in the Dominion. As far as Lord Stanley was concerned, the trophy was to be known as the Dominion Hockey Challenge Cup, but it soon took on the name of its benefactor.

To this donation of a trophy he added a few strings, the most important of which was that the cup was to be played for each year by as many amateur hockey teams as the trustees of the trophy considered appropriate. As a result, in the early years teams representing a total of 17 different amateur leagues attempted to capture Lord Stanley's esteemed hardware.

The very first recipient of the new trophy was the Montreal Amateur Athletic Association, which won it in 1893. For the next 17 years the prize was played for by both amateur and professional teams. Then, from 1910 on, only professional hockey teams, including those in the newly established National Hockey Association (NHA), competed for the Stanley Cup.

The NHA initially consisted of teams from such communities as Montreal, Quebec, Renfrew, Cobalt, and Haileybury. Then, in 1912, a

The 1914 Torontos, the first Toronto club to win the Stanley Cup. Standing left to right: R. Carroll, trainer; C. Corbeau, defence; "Minnie" McGiffen, wing; Jack Marshall, point and manager; George McNamara, defence; Jack Walker, rover; C.W. Wilson, wing; F. Carroll, trainer. Seated: Cully Wilson, goal; Frank Foyston, centre; "Scotty" Davidson, defence and coach; Harry Cameron, cover point; Harry Holmes, goal.

couple of new franchises were awarded, both to Toronto. However, when it became apparent that the proposed $500,000 Arena Gardens on Mutual Street in which the two teams would play their respective home games wouldn't be ready in time, both teams — the Torontos and the Tecumsehs — had to wait until the following season before joining the NHA.

The Torontos went on to win the NHA title for the 1913–14 season. As was the custom back in those days, the Stanley Cup would then be awarded to the winner of a best-of-five-game playoff between the NHA champions, the Torontos (who were also referred to in some stories as the Blueshirts and Ontarios) and the Victoria Cougars, the Pacific Coast Hockey League champions. The boys from Toronto took the 1913–14 Stanley Cup after defeating Victoria 5–2, 6–5, and 2–1. This was the first time a Toronto club appeared on Lord Stanley's trophy. By the way, in the first game one of the Victoria players was benched for "loafing."

In 1917–18 victory happened again when the team, now called the Arenas, defeated the Vancouver Millionaires. Four years later the Toronto team under another new name, the St. Pats, once again beat Vancouver. Both these triumphs came under manager Charlie Querrie (who died in 1950 and is buried in Mount Pleasant Cemetery). The coaches in 1917–18 and 1921–22 were Dick Carroll (trainer of the very first Toronto Stanley Cup victors) and Eddie Powers respectively.

It wasn't until the 1931–32 season that the name Toronto Maple Leafs, the new moniker of the St. Pats since 1927, first appeared on the Stanley Cup. The owner and manager was Conn Smythe, with Dick Irvin as coach. The latter passed away in 1957 and is also in Mount Pleasant Cemetery (as is the coach of the last Leafs Stanley Cup team, George "Punch" Imlach, who died in 1987). Since that first Maple Leafs Cup victory in 1932, the team has won Lord Stanley's trophy another 10 times, the last occasion being in 1967.

May 2, 2004

History Loves a Hero

The Toronto fire of April 19 to 20, 1904, destroyed more than 100 buildings in a 20-acre area bounded by (approximately) King, Yonge, the Esplanade, and York. It was finally extinguished by exhausted fire crews from Toronto and several surrounding communities, but smoke still filled the air and small fires continued to erupt in the piles of rubble.

The conflagration, which was to enter the history books (where it remains to this day) as the worst in the city's history, had many unsung heroes in addition to those who actually fought the fire. John Johnston was one of them. Johnston was born in Cannington, Ontario, in 1856 and came to Toronto shortly after the turn of the 20th century. He soon obtained employment as a night watchman, with his assigned patrol area the blocks bordered by Simcoe, Wellington, Scott, and Front streets, a district within downtown Toronto that was packed with warehouses full of items ranging from clothing materials and paper products to leather goods and printing supplies.

In the months and years that followed the fire, Johnston often related how, on the evening of April 19, 1904, as he walked along the south side of Wellington Street not far from the Bay corner, he saw the reflection of fire in the lane alongside the old Currie Building at 58 Wellington West. He went to investigate and, finding the flames leaping up the elevator shaft, ran up to Bay Street and there turned in

The northwest corner of Bay and Wellington streets after the Great Toronto Fire of 1904.

Box Number 12 on which the Great Fire was rung in by John Johnston on April 19, 1904. This alarm box is still in the possession of the Toronto Fire Department.

the alarm using Box Number 12 located at the northeast corner of King Street. Johnston returned to the scene of the fire, and in the darkness of the laneway stumbled over some hot bricks that had fallen from the crumbling wall. He was badly burned about the hands and forehead.

Johnston would go on to relate how the flames leaped from one old brick warehouse to another, the narrow lanes between them offering no resistance to the fire's progress. No defence either was the material out of which the interiors of the structures were built. Wooden floors and joists quickly caught fire, and without the structural support they afforded, the walls eventually collapsed in on themselves or out onto streets such as Bay, Wellington, and Front. Falling outwards, the walls brought down telephone, telegraph, and overhead streetcar lines and in doing so enveloped much of downtown Toronto in a spider's web of crackling and sputtering wires.

Final resting place in Mount Pleasant Cemetery of John Johnston, the night watchman who turned in the alarm alerting Torontonians that their city was on fire.

As the city rebuilt itself, John Johnston returned to his duties and continued to patrol downtown Toronto for nearly 17 more years. In his 30-year career he turned in a total of 57 alarms, none as memorable as the one he reported on that cold, windy night in April 1904.

Johnston died on January 26, 1921, and is buried in Mount Pleasant Cemetery.

May 9, 2004

Streetcars on Parade

The 2004 Toronto Easter Parade followed a route along Queen Street through the Beaches district of the city. Watched by thousands, this annual event has been sponsored for many years by the extremely active Beaches Lions Club. (Okay, let's get it out of the way. Historically, it's "Beach," since in the beginning the area was one long, sandy beach. Today the term *Beaches* is used to refer to the pair of beaches, Kew and Balmy, plus other small unnamed beaches that have developed along the water's edge in more recent times.)

Unusual participants in the parade for the past few years are three Toronto Transit Commission streetcars, one of which is a "relic" from the days when a ride on this type of vehicle was seven cents cash for adults (four tickets for 25 cents), with a child's fare (determined by an ever-increasing height limit and not age) set at three cents. The vehicle I'm referring to is the Peter Witt streetcar, a name given to this particular model in recognition of its designer, Mr. Peter Witt, a well-respected transportation expert who practised his profession for many years in Cleveland, Ohio.

Over the years the TTC operated a total of 575 "Large," "Small," and trailer versions of the Witt car. The "Small" Witt that appeared in the parade, number 2766, has been lovingly restored to its 1923 state by craftspeople of the TTC and is the last of its kind on the commission's streetcar roster. The fleet also includes a pair of restored 1951

Two Toronto "landmarks": the Toronto Transit Commission's beautifully restored 1923 "Small" Peter Witt streetcar number 2766 and the 1854 Ashbridge House on Queen Street East.

Most of the TTC's Peter Witt cars weren't as fortunate as number 2766. In this 1957 photograph "Large" Peter Witt number 2978 meets its fate at a Cherry Street wrecking yard.

PCC cars, one of which was also in the parade. Incidentally, the PCCs are available for private charter (information from the TTC Charter Office at 416-393-7880). Daily streetcar service is provided by 196 CLRVs plus 52 of the larger articulated version (ALRV) of this Canadian-designed vehicle.

Returning to its home at the TTC's Harvey Shops at Bathurst and Davenport, the Witt stopped for a short visit with another city icon, the Ashbridge House on the north side of Queen Street just east of Greenwood Avenue.

The house was erected in 1854 on property that had been acquired by Sarah Ashbridge soon after she arrived in York (renamed Toronto in 1834) from Pennsylvania many years before. It was Sarah's son, Jesse, who built what was originally a single-storey farmhouse on the eastern outskirts of the 20-year-old City of Toronto. Twenty years after Jesse's death in 1874 his wife, Elizabeth, began to modernize the old family residence, adding such things as hot-water heating, gas lighting, and a second floor that gave the house its present appearance.

Two more generations of the Ashbridge family lived in the house: Wellington Ashbridge (son of Jesse and Elizabeth) from 1919 to 1952, followed by daughters, Betty and Dorothy, who inherited the house from their parents.

Ashbridge House was preserved for all Ontarians when, in 1972, Betty and Dorothy donated the residence to the Ontario Heritage Foundation in whose care this historic structure rests today.

May 16, 2004

Location, Location, Location

T he three views accompanying this column were all taken from similar vantage points on the east side of Yonge Street just south of the Queen corner. One building is common to all three photos and it still stands on the northwest corner of the intersection. Built in 1895 by Philip Jamieson to house his very popular men's clothing business, the then new building replaced on the same site the structure that was badly damaged when Robert Simpson's department store across the street (now the site of the Hudson's Bay store) was gutted by fire earlier that same year.

Examining the photos in the set, we see that in photo number 1 the store has become the home of S.H. Knox & Company, a five-and-dime emporium. That happened soon after Mr. Jamieson's death in 1909. The next view shows it as a Woolworth's store, a change that occurred in 1912. The present-day photo reveals that Jamieson's building is now the home of Coast Mountain Sports.

As for the dates of the photos, determining them is part of the fun in writing this column. As mentioned, Frank Woolworth moved into his nephew Seymour Horace Knox's place in 1912. Combine that with the fact that the Jamieson business vanished after the clothier's death in February 1909, therefore, photo number 1 must have been taken between 1909 and 1912.

The second view is somewhat easier to date, thanks to the cars present. In the right foreground is a 1962 Pontiac with what appears to

Yonge Street looking north to Queen Street, circa 1910, 1965, and 2004.

be a licence plate with white letters, a dark background, and six digits. A little research on the Internet tells us the year 1965 would be a possible match for this type of plate, which suggests that was also the year the photo was taken.

Photo number 3 was taken in April 2004 and I should know. I took it.

May 23, 2004

Tragic Loss

E arly on the morning of May 29, 1914, Canadian Pacific's trans-atlantic passenger liner *Empress of Ireland* sank in the cold waters of the St. Lawrence River after colliding with the Norwegian-registered coal freighter *Storstad*. It was the worst marine disaster in Canadian history.

The *Empress* was constructed in the Fairfield Engineering Company's shipyard in Govan, Scotland, in 1906. Prior to departing the dock at Quebec City at 4:27 on the afternoon of May 28, 1914, the ship had completed a total of 95 successful transatlantic crossings. On board the first leg of the 96th trip were 1,057 passengers and 420 crew for a total complement of 1,477 souls. Included in the passenger manifest was a large contingent of Salvation Army members from the Toronto area who were accompanied by wives, children, and friends, all of whom were bound for the army's International Congress being held in London, England. Among the Salvationists were 41 members of the army's celebrated Canadian Staff Band who were eagerly looking forward to performing at the important event.

The trip started out as had every previous crossing — smoothly and without incident. Soon night enveloped the vessel and all was quiet as the *Empress* made its way downriver in the inky blackness towards the Atlantic Ocean. Then, at exactly 1:35 a.m., several of the crew on the liner's bridge spotted the lights of another ship well in the distance. It was obvious from the positioning of the navigational lights that the craft was headed upriver.

The *Empress's* captain, Henry Kendall, was notified, and he quickly determined that there was plenty of room for the two vessels to pass each other in safety. However, just to be sure, Kendall altered course to increase the distance between the ships. Suddenly, both the *Empress* and the *Storstad* were enveloped in thick fog. Now both captains were blind, and without the benefit of radio or radar only the sound of the ships' whistles provided the assistance necessary to locate each other in the impenetrable murkiness.

The tragic sinking of the Canadian Pacific liner *Empress of Ireland* in 1914 holds the dubious distinction of being Canada's worst maritime disaster.

But it wasn't enough. Just when both captains believed they were performing the proper manoeuvres, the two vessels collided, the *Storstad's* knife-like bow slicing deep into the starboard side of the *Empress* amidships, a deep and mortal wound that would result in the liner slipping into oblivion, along with more than a thousand of her passengers and crew in a mere 14 minutes.

Interestingly, the passenger death toll resulting from the relatively unknown *Empress of Ireland* disaster exceeded by 33 the number of passengers lost when the *Titanic* went to the bottom a little more

The *Empress of Ireland* memorial monument in Mount Pleasant Cemetery continues to be the site of commemorative services on the last Sunday in May.

than two years earlier. Among the victims were 167 Salvationists, including 29 members of the Toronto-based Staff Band.

May 30, 2004

Royal Site

I n the Canadian Pacific Railway Annual Report for the year 1926, the following statement appears:

> Your Directors, after careful consideration, have decided that it is very much in the interests of the Company to erect a hotel in the City of Toronto, where the hotel accommodation is quite inadequate to meet the commercial and tourist traffic which centers in that important city. The Board has considered such a hotel for some time, but had refrained from asking the shareholders for their approval in view of the extensive expenditures to which the company was committed in Quebec City, Regina, Lake Louise and Banff. Now, however, that the major portion of the works in connection with these hotels has been completed or is approaching completion your Directors feel that the construction of a hotel in Toronto should not be longer delayed.

And with that official statement laid out for all to see, work soon began on the construction of what would be the largest hotel not just in Toronto, or in Canada, but in the entire British Commonwealth.

Soon after, in the March 1927 edition of *Contract Record and Engineering Review* magazine, the architects responsible for the look of the new hotel were announced. In fact, it would be a team effort using the talents of the Montreal firm of Ross & Macdonald with Toronto's Sproat and Rolph serving as associate architects.

Actually, this wasn't the first time a CPR hotel for Toronto was the topic of discussion. As early as 1906, rumours flew that the Bank of Montreal would move from the corner of Yonge and Front streets (a building that now houses the Hockey Hall of Fame) into a new building at the northeast corner of Yonge and Queen (the facade of which has been beautifully restored). CPR would then build a new hotel on the Yonge and Front property as well as on the lot occupied by the Minerva Building to the west. The plan turned out to be just that — a rumour.

The stately Royal York Hotel soon after its official opening in 1929. A 400-room addition would be erected 30 years later to the east of the hotel, right where those lovely old cars are parked in this view. A Witt streetcar on the Yonge route rumbles by in front of the hotel.

Two decades later the CPR hotel idea finally became reality. This time, though, the site it would occupy would be farther west — the entire block bounded by Front, York, Piper, and a new street that would be created to the east of the hotel. It was anticipated that this last thoroughfare, to be called Federal Avenue, would be laid out as a grand boulevard connecting Front Street with Queen Street at a point opposite the site of Toronto's "New" City Hall.

Federal Avenue never got off the drawing board for a variety of reasons, including the supposition that the new street was being built to enhance the value of the recently constructed *Toronto Star* Building on King Street between Bay and York. True or not, the mere hint that there might be something inappropriate going on was enough to get the other Toronto newspapers to print impassioned stories against the project. It wasn't long before the proposed Federal Avenue was yesterday's news.

Of course, the primary reason the Front Street site was selected was because of its proximity to the city's new Union Station. Interestingly, though the new station was pretty much ready for business at the time the new hotel announcement was first made in 1926, it was still closed to the public because of an ongoing disagreement about the final alignment of the tracks serving the new station and who would pay the enormous costs of that project. As it turned out, another half-year would pass after the hotel's opening before the new station was declared fully operational.

Crews clear the site on which the new Royal York Hotel will be constructed. The wooden streetcar in the foreground is on the Bathurst route (St. Clair Avenue and Vaughan Road via Vaughan, Bathurst, and Front to loop at Frederick) and sits westbound at the Front and York intersection, November 18, 1927.

Once the station opened, however, it would be easy for train travellers to get to and from the hotel thanks to the pedestrian tunnel constructed under Front Street. That tunnel, along with the one that used to connect the old Eaton's store with its Annex, were "pioneers" in the city's present 16.8-mile-long underground walkway system (PATH).

The new $16-million, 1,100-room hotel was officially opened on June 11, 1929, by Viscount Willingdon, Canada's governor general of the day.

In 2004, to honour the Fairmont Royal York Hotel's 75th anniversary, the treasured Toronto landmark was presented with an Ontario Heritage Foundation blue-and-gold commemorative plaque.

June 6, 2004

It's a Gas, Gas, Gas

When I was going to Ryerson Polytechnical Institute back in the last century, one of my great delights was working at the late Harry Norman's BP gas station at the corner of Mount Pleasant Road and Belsize. Actually, the term *working* is a bit misleading, since that conjures up the idea of money changing hands and Harry never paid me a nickel. Not that he didn't want to; it's just that I helped him out in exchange for having access to the station's hydraulic hoist (so I could change my own oil or rotate the tires), the chain-driven wash rack (where I could wash my 1958 Hillman Minx, of particular value in the depths of winters that were much colder back then), and the treasure trove of specialty car tools essential for fixing this or adjusting that, particularly if the this or that was on an English car like mine — you know, the ones that if it even looked like rain, they wouldn't start.

I had known Harry for several years ever since I bought my first car (that %^$#^* Hillman) from the Rootes dealership that he and the late Jan Wietzes (later the Wietzes of Wietzes Motors on north Yonge Street) ran out of a little Supertest station on the northeast corner of Mount Pleasant Road and Broadway Avenue.

There I am monkeying with the truth again. The Hillman wasn't really my first car. Nope, that was a 1949 Morris Minor that cost me $75. And to refer to it (with its mechanical brakes, plastic stick-on windshield defroster panels, and eye-catching do-it-yourself turquoise

215

Looking north on Mount Pleasant Road at Merton Street, circa 1941. Note the horse-drawn bread wagon crossing Mount Pleasant, the PCC streetcar on the St. Clair route (operating from the loop at Eglinton south to St. Clair Avenue, west to Weston Road, north to the loop at Northland Avenue). Also visible is a trio of gas stations: BA (above and behind the streetcar at Davisville Avenue), Sunoco (to the extreme left of the view), and McColl-Frontenac to the right.

There's only one gas station in this same view taken in 2004.

paint job completed with a cheap two-inch brush in the driveway of the Filey residence on nearby Elvina Gardens) as a car was stretching a point.

What I remember most about the days when I worked — played — in Harry's station was the number of other gas stations along Mount Pleasant Road. Starting at Merton Street, I can remember a Sunoco and Texaco on the northwest and northeast corners respectively, a BA at the southwest corner of Davisville, Harry's BP at the southwest corner of Belsize, McConnell's Texaco station on the west side north of Soudan, another BA at the northeast corner of Mount Pleasant and Eglinton, a Supertest at Broadway, another BA at the southwest corner of Erskine, a Shell station at the southwest corner of Keewatin, an Imperial station at the southeast corner of Sherwood, and Jack Marr's place at Stibbard. Now let's see. Nearly a dozen gas stations in a 13-block stretch? I wonder … more choices, more competition, better prices?

Today your choice is limited to the Esso station (which was McColl-Frontenac, as in the photo, then Texaco) at Merton.

Actually, until last month there were two stations still in business, but that number was halved when Wally Clayson's Shell station at Keewatin closed. Wally got into the business in the 1950s (and first skinned his knuckles on cars like my 1955 Pontiac) in what was originally a White Rose station. This Canadian company was bought out by the international Shell organization and operated as such until last month when the place closed with the site soon to be covered by another condominium tower.

No fear, though. Wally, assisted by his team members Steve, Tom, and Craig, now operates the Master Mechanic franchise on Laird Drive in Leaside.

June 13, 2004

In the Eye of a Camera

There was a time when I thought I would never stoop to using a digital camera. I had always relied on a 35 mm camera and was pretty sure that good digital cameras were only for the rich and probably wouldn't catch on, anyway.

Well, someone convinced me to try one, and while I won't give up my Olympus OM-2 film camera any time soon, I am more than happy with my new HP R707 digital camera. One thing: if you're going to go digital, get as many megapixels as you can afford the first time around. Upgrading is expensive.

The two photos that accompany this column were captured using totally different imaging technologies. The first was printed from an "ancient" glass plate negative while the modern-day view was created digitally. The former took time to process while the latter, with the right equipment, was produced almost instantaneously.

In the earlier view the newly constructed Bank of Montreal is to the extreme left of the photo. A portion of the same building, now the site of the Hockey Hall of Fame, appears in the modern-day view. In the centre background a few of the old buildings at the southwest corner of Yonge and Wellington streets can be seen in both views, though today only the "ancient" facades remain in place. To the extreme right of the older photo is a portion of the American Hotel where Charles Dickens stayed during his 1842 visit to Toronto. Note

Looking north on Yonge Street from Front Street, circa 1890.

The same view in 2004.

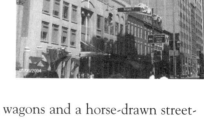

the presence of several horse-drawn wagons and a horse-drawn street-car travelling up Yonge Street.

Towering in the background of the modern view are (left to right) First Canadian Place (the tallest building in Canada), the top of the Bank of Commerce Building (once the British Empire's tallest building), and Scotia Plaza. The building under construction is Harry Stinson's new condo tower adjacent to 1 King Street West.

June 20, 2004

It's Jolly Miller Time

The Ontario Municipal Board has approved the construction of a 54-suite motor hotel to replace the Jolly Miller
Hotel on Yonge Street at Mill Street in North York. The
decision was made after the Metropolitan Toronto
Planning Board withdrew its request for a postponement of
the rezoning application. The Planning Board had requested the deferment until the route of the Yonge subway
extension had been decided. The Board said that the Jolly
Miller was involved in only one of the proposed routes
through Hogg's Hollow and that a decision on which route
would be followed was far in the future

The above item appeared in a Toronto newspaper on April 22,
1962. Interestingly, there was virtually no uproar about the
potential loss of the Jolly Miller, a landmark on north Yonge Street
since circa 1857 when it was built to replace an earlier structure that
was destroyed by fire. Originally called the York Mills Hotel, the new
building was erected by John and William Hogg, who had recently
subdivided their father's property for building sites (one of the first
such land-use projects in the Toronto region). The Hogg brothers
then built a general store next door to the hotel (the former was
destroyed by fire in 1978), and together the two buildings became the

220

Artist's sketch showing what was going on inside the Jolly Miller just prior to a police raid on the purported gambling den. The sketch accompanied a 1934 *Telegram* newspaper story outlining why the raid failed.

The Jolly Miller on Yonge Street in Hogg's Hollow still stands and recently reopened as the Miller Tavern.

focal point for the surrounding community and the various mills that had developed along the Don River where the swift-flowing waters were used to spin the grindstones (one of which can still be seen at the corner of Donino Avenue and Plymbridge Road).

Over the years the old hotel went through a number of name changes as well as uses. In fact, during the years of liquor prohibition (1916 to 1927), the place became a notorious gambling den and was often the subject of raids by officers of the provincial police force.

In recent years the Jolly Miller served as both a hotel and tavern, and while the hotel part ceased operations in 1964, there are still many around who remember downing a cool one at the Jolly Miller. Now, as the Miller Tavern, the landmark building is ready to serve a new generation of visitors.

Oh, by the way, there's a reference in that 1962 newspaper article to the route for the extension of the Yonge subway being far in the future. They weren't kidding. The 2.7-mile-long stretch from Eglinton to York Mills didn't open for another 11 years!

* * *

The Halton County Radial Railway Museum, located on the Guelph Line north of Highway 401 (take Exit 312), celebrated its 50th anniversary in 2004. It all started when a few transit enthusiasts banded together to save the Toronto Transit Commission's last wooden streetcar. A site for an operating museum was found, and with the co-operation of the TTC, the nucleus of what would become one of the continent's largest and most active operating streetcar museums was eventually opened to the public. Come take a ride on an old-fashioned streetcar. For all details see *www.hcry.org*.

June 27, 2004

Ride the Trade Winds

My "In the Eye of a Camera" column from June 20, 2004, featured a photo of Yonge Street looking north from Front. In it there appeared a portion of the old American Hotel that stood on the northeast corner of that intersection. This was the same hotel in which the famed Charles Dickens stayed during his brief visit to Toronto in early May 1842. As the young city matured, the land on which the hotel sat became increasingly valuable, and in November 1887 the site, along with another smaller parcel of land on Front Street just east of Yonge, was purchased by the Toronto Board of Trade for $69,500.

Established in 1845 (just three years after Dickens's visit), this organization was created to express the views of the city's business community on matters pertaining to trade, railway development, and tariffs as well as to help protect the interests of the community in general. As the city grew, the board realized its responsibilities had also grown, so much so that its facilities in the old Imperial Bank Building at the corner of Wellington and Leader Lane had become totally inadequate. Officers of the board decided to erect a new structure in the heart of the business community, and the site on which the old, and by now rather archaic, American Hotel stood was selected.

In an interesting turn of events the board, which supposedly represented purely local interests, decided that the design completion for the new building would be open to both Canadian and American

The Board of Trade Building, northeast corner of Yonge and Front streets. While the photo is undated, the year it was taken can be determined using the presence of the horse-drawn streetcar on Yonge Street, the clothing worn by the pedestrians, and the fact that the building was officially occupied in late 1890. The horse cars were replaced by electric cars in September 1892, therefore the photo must have been snapped in the warmer months of either 1891 or 1892.

The same view in 2004.

architects. This decision, as one can imagine, stirred up much controversy. Feelings finally boiled over when it was announced that of the three finalists in the competition, two Canadian and one American, the American submission was chosen. And then it was revealed that the supposedly secret identities of the competitors were actually known before the final selection. Things then really hit the fan. Newspapers and politicians had a field day.

Nevertheless, the American-based firm of English architects, James and James, went to work on the project. The American Hotel was demolished and the new building began to take shape. But as the late Bill Dendy describes in his marvellous book *Lost Toronto* (Oxford University Press), the troubles had just started. First the structure suffered a partial collapse when one of the support beams snapped under the weight of bricks. The city then declared the rest of the building unsafe, resulting in the architect firing the builder followed by the Board of Trade firing the architects. Then a local builder was hired to complete the project. The most obvious outcome of the fiasco was the cost overruns that pushed the new building's construction more than $140,000 over the original $200,000 budget. The board was not pleased.

The impressive, if expensive, structure was finally ready for occupancy in the 1890, with the board moving into its new offices on the top floor. There the board remained until 1914 when another relocation saw it move into the Royal Bank Building, the city's new skyscraper up the street at King.

Many Torontonians will remember the building as the head office of the Toronto Transit Commission. The TTC remained in the Board of Trade Building until shortly before the structure's demolition in the late 1950s. The site then became a parking lot, and so it remained for more than 20 years until the present structure, known by the rather nondescript title of 33 Yonge Street, was built. On October 1, 1982, 33 Yonge Street was officially opened by John B. Aird, Ontario's lieutenant governor.

July 4, 2004

Madison Square Garden in Toronto

Anyone walking along Richmond Street in downtown Toronto recently (before the original publication of this column on July 11, 2004) could have been excused if they thought they had been swept back in time in some sort of infernal machine and had come to a stop in downtown New York City sometime in the 1930s. For there, on the north side of the street, where The Bay store was and just steps west of Yonge, was New York's famed Madison Square Garden, flanked by several stores, including Harmony Records, Adam's Hats, and Florsheim Shoes. And over there shops that were also popular in Toronto back then — a United Cigar Store and next to it a Liggett's drugstore. Why, I can remember when I was a kid there was a Liggett's at the northwest corner of Bloor and Bathurst. It and several other Liggett stores in the city were bought out by Gordon Tamblyn and soon became part of his chain of drugstores.

And there, running in front of the Garden, was a pair of old-fashioned streetcars identified as part of the Third Avenue Railway on its "Broadway" route. What was going on?

Well, as I'm sure many readers know by now, the buildings, including the Madison Square Garden's overhanging marquee, were simply facades constructed to convert a portion of Richmond Street West into the streetscape in front of the Garden during the time that boxer James J. Braddock (1906–1974) fought his way into the history books, defeating Max Baer in 1935 to become the world heavyweight champion. His last

Richmond Street West, just west of Yonge, sports a nostalgic marquee from the 1930s as it represents New York City in the movie *Cinderella Man*.

victory was at Madison Square Garden three years later. Braddock's rise from virtual obscurity to world champion earned him the nickname "Cinderella Man."

A motion picture documenting Braddock's story and titled, not surprisingly, *Cinderella Man* was being filmed at various locations in Toronto. The movie stars Russell Crowe as Braddock.

Oh, and those two Peter Witt streetcars (so named for the American designer of the car) rumbling through the scene? Number 2766 belongs to the TTC, and the other, number 2894, was trucked into town from the Halton County Radial Railway Museum west of the city near Guelph. Both cars were built by the Ottawa Car Company in 1923 and were part of the TTC's extensive Peter Witt fleet that included 100 of the "Small" version and 250 of the "Large" Peter Witts that were longer, wider, and had a higher passenger-carrying capacity. In the part of the film that's supposed to be in Hoboken, New Jersey, where Braddock scored his first knockout in 1926, the museum's "Large" Witt number 2424 (built in 1921) is featured, complete with an orange livery to simulate one of that American city's streetcars.

July 11, 2004

Blazing a Trail

On July 21, 1965, the freighter SS *Orient Trader* was loaded with, among other things, a huge cargo of rubber when it caught fire while berthed at Toronto's Pier 11, just east of the foot of Yonge Street. Arriving on the scene 90 seconds after receiving the alarm, the fire department's fireboat *William Lyon Mackenzie* (named after Toronto's first mayor, who appropriately enough was often described as a "fiery Scot") was soon pouring thousands of gallons of water on the burning vessel. Once crews could get close enough to tie lines onto the vessel, *Mackenzie* hauled the stricken ship away from the nearby warehouses, thereby removing the threat of having the adjacent waterfront erupt in flames. With the *Orient Trader* now out of the way, the fireboat continued to douse the flames and in the process saved nearly a quarter of a million dollars of cargo stored in other areas of the burning ship. Fire Chief Charles Chambers said that the presence of the fireboat had saved not only the pier, but much of the rest of the waterfront, as well.

Since the fireboat's arrival from the Russel Brothers shipyard in Owen Sound on May 15, 1964, the *Mackenzie* had been the subject of much controversy, most of it sparked by some City Council members who could see no need for such a craft. In fact, as far as "they" were concerned, it was a "boondoggle," perpetrated on the citizens of Toronto by the previous council. "They" would be more careful about how the poor taxpayer's money would be spent.

Launching ceremonies at Russel Brothers shipyard in Owen Sound, November 7, 1963, for Toronto's new fireboat *William Lyon Mackenzie*. At the podium is Mayor Don Summerville, who would die of a massive heart attack less than two weeks later.

The recently refurbished *William Lyon Mackenzie*, now 40 years old, is still amazingly active.

Now with fire and insurance officials agreeing that the *Mackenzie* had saved the city millions in potential damages to its waterfront structures, the year-old fireboat had been vindicated.

Actually, the idea of acquiring a proper fireboat for the protection of ships, personnel, and property along the city's waterfront had first been talked about even while the search continued for more victims on board SS *Noronic*, the Canada Steamship Line's cruise boat that burned alongside Pier 9 at the foot of Yonge Street on September 17, 1949. It was obvious that the *Charles Reed*, a small pleasure craft converted for firefighting duties, was useless when it came to fighting or even containing a fire of any significant size.

It wasn't until the council under Mayor Nathan Phillips approved an expenditure of $600,000 that anything was done to get the city its fireboat. *Mackenzie* was christened by City Council member Mary Temple on November 7, 1963. The new vessel was then fitted out, underwent trials, and arrived in Toronto Harbour on May 15 of the following year.

Recently, Toronto's fireboat underwent a major refitting and upgrading at the Toronto Drydock Company yard at the east end of the harbour. Not long ago, *Mackenzie* was called on to assist in fighting the flames that destroyed the Island Yacht Club building on Mugg's Island. There is some speculation that without the presence of the "new and improved" fireboat all of Mugg's Island, most of which is a bird sanctuary, might have been lost.

In addition to its firefighting role, the *Mackenzie* also performs ice-breaking duties in the winter months, has water pollution containment capabilities, and assists in search-and-rescue operations. The boat is often called upon to welcome visiting dignitaries or perform at various waterfront festivities.

July 18, 2004

Welcome to the Neighbourhood

The *Toronto Sun* has a new neighbour. In fact, we have a lot of new neighbours now that the men and women of Toronto Police Service's 51 Division have moved into their new digs at the northeast corner of Front and Parliament streets. While the building has a fascinating history, so, too, does the division itself. Established in 1870, 4 Division, as it was originally called, operated out of a building on the north side of Dundas Street just east of Parliament. The division's boundaries were Bloor Street to the north, the waterfront to the south, and all the streets between the Don River on the east and Jarvis Street on the west. The "ancient" Dundas Street building served until a new facility opened on Regent Street in 1956. Built at a cost of $400,000 and touted in one of the newspapers of the day as a "dazzler," this station, too, soon became badly overcrowded.

It was decided that another new home for the division would be built, and after numerous meetings it was agreed the new station would be located at the northeast corner of Front and Parliament streets and that a portion of the Consumers' Gas Building, which had been designated in 1978 under the Ontario Heritage Act as a structure of both architectural and historic merit, would be incorporated into the new layout as created by Toronto's Dunlop Architects, Incorporated.

As to the origins of the old building, it was built in 1899–1900 and was a key component of Consumers' Gas's sprawling Station A.

Aerial view of the old Consumers' Gas complex in and around the corner of Front and Parliament streets. The part of the Purifying House that was incorporated into the Toronto Police Service's new 51 Division is behind the chimney to the left of the view. The street to the extreme left is Parliament, and the view looks north, circa 1930.

The Toronto Police Service's new 51 Division, northeast corner of Front and Parliament streets.

The building housed the purifying operations associated with the manufacture of coal gas that was used primarily for manufacturing and cooking purposes throughout the city of nearly 200,000 people. The process worked like this. Every day boatloads of Pennsylvanian coal would arrive at the Consumers' Gas dock near the foot of Parliament Street. From there the coal was conveyed by wagon to the retort house at the southeast corner of Front and Berkeley where it was burned at high temperatures. This procedure resulted in two products — coke and coal gas — with the former being sold for use in home stoves and the latter transferred to the Purifying House (a portion of which is now home to 51 Division) where sulphur, nitrous oxides, tar, and many other impurities were removed. The scrubbed coal gas was then sent to the huge gas holders, also called gasometers, located on the south side of Front Street. Two of them, with a third under construction, can be seen in the accompanying photo. The gas would then be distributed from these holders to the company's customers around town.

An interesting feature of the gasometer was its "floating roof" that would rise as the gas was being pumped in and fall as the gas was being withdrawn. With the arrival in 1954 of natural gas from Texas and subsequently from western Canada, the need for this process ceased and the buildings were eventually abandoned by Consumers' Gas. Two of the buildings are used for theatrical and operatic purposes with a third now housing those who "serve and protect."

July 25, 2004

Promenade to the Past

O f the various types of articles I prepare for this column, those that use "then and now" photos seem to be the most popular. That's no doubt because most readers can recognize the modern-day view, making it easier for them to comprehend the older view and the changes time has impressed upon our city. Of all the old photos and sketches I've come across, one of the best for doing "then and now" appears in a book the City of Toronto commissioned in celebration of its 150th anniversary.

The author was Edith Firth, an expert on the history of early Toronto, who selected over 170 views depicting the city from its inception in 1834 to the present day. In one of the views she chose, artist John Gillespie shows us King Street looking west from Jarvis in the year 1844. At that time King was the 10-year-old city's main drag as is exemplified by the number of shops and stores in the view as well as by the parade of pedestrians, a gathering that includes two soldiers from the 93rd Regiment of Foot in full dress uniform. The building at the extreme left was part of the original St. Lawrence Market and housed the young city's council chamber on its upper floor. Most of this building was destroyed in a fire that swept the area in April 1849. Another structure that succumbed to the flames was the 1839 version of St. James's Cathedral, the spire of which can be seen in the background.

August 1, 2004

King Street looking west from Jarvis Street by John Gillespie, circa 1844 (from *Toronto in Art* by Edith Firth, Fitzhenry & Whiteside, 1983).

A similar view in 2004.

Talk About Gas Pain

In view of the rising price of gasoline, I don't know whether the accompanying photos will make you feel nostalgic or just mad. The first shows a nattily attired White Rose service station attendant filling the tank of a 1960 Pontiac. Under a magnifying glass the regular gas is 41.9 cents a gallon while the ultra is four cents a gallon more.

The origin of the White Rose brand of gasoline goes back to 1901 when the Canadian Oil Company was formed in Petrolia, Ontario. To combat pressures inflicted on the Canadian market by several gasoline conglomerates south of the border, the Canadian company joined forces with eight other local petroleum businesses to form Canadian Oil Limited. Unfortunately, this new firm failed, and in 1907 it was purchased by the National Refining Company of Cleveland, Ohio. The effects of the Great Depression eventually forced the American company to sell most of its assets to the Montreal-based Nesbitt, Thomson and Company, an international securities firm that had, among other things, established the Power Corporation of Canada in 1925.

It was under Nesbitt, Thomson management that the White Rose brand of gasoline first appeared. White Rose gas was marketed for more than a quarter of a century before it was bought out by Shell Oil Company of Canada, itself part of the Royal Dutch Shell group.

In the other photograph a mini-skirted assistant describes to a customer just how Esso's new "self-service" gas stations work. Briefly,

Filling 'er up at a White Rose station in the fall of 1962.

In the spring of 1970, Esso opened its first "self-service" stations with the one in this view at Eglinton Avenue and Brimley Road.

the customer used an intercom to tell the female attendant in a sepa-rate booth how much gasoline he wished and helped himself. I can only assume he helped himself to the gasoline and not to the atten-dant, though the wording is somewhat ambiguous. He then went to the booth and paid the attendant. When this promotional photo was taken in 1970, the price per gallon of regular gas had risen from 41.9 cents in 1962 to 47.9 cents. I know it's unfair to compare 1970 prices with today's, but what the heck … that 47.9 cents would work out to 10.6 cents a litre.

* * *

October 15, 2004, marks the 50th anniversary of Hurricane Hazel's unwelcome visit to Toronto. To try to ensure that the death and dev-astation left in the storm's wake never happened again, an organization known as the Metropolitan Toronto and Region Conservation Authority was established. Over time its mandate expanded from floodplain management to encompass all aspects of balance between the human and natural elements in the city. The fascinating story of the MTRCA (now TRCA) and the organization's impact on this part of a very diverse world can be found in a new book titled *Paths to the Living City* by Bill McLean, a senior official with the TRCA until his retirement in 1992. It's not available in stores, but anyone interested in purchasing a copy is invited to visit *trca.on.ca/paths* or phone 416-661-6600 and ask for Customer Service.

August 8, 2004